We're all smiles,
then honest I swear
it's the turnstiles
that make us hostile.

- ***We'll let you know*** : **Morrissey**

THE FAMILY GAME

The untold story of hooliganism in Rugby League

by Michael James

The Parrs Wood Press
<u>Manchester</u>

First Published 2005

This book is copyright under the Berne Convention. All rights are reserved. Apart from any fair dealing for the purpose of private study, research, criticism or review, as permitted under the Copyright Act 1956, no part of this publication may be reproduced, stored in a retrieval system, or transmitted in any form or by any means electronic, electrical, chemical, mechanical, optical, photocopying, recording or otherwise without the prior permission of the copyright owner. Enquiries should be sent to the publisher at the undermentioned address.

THE PARRS WOOD PRESS
St Wilfrid's Enterprise Centre
Royce Road, Manchester, M15 5BJ
www.parrswoodpress.com

© Michael James 2005

ISBN: 1 903158 62 1

Printed by Biddles Ltd of King's Lynn

CONTENTS

Preface

SITTING IN THE sell-out, almost 70,000-strong crowd at Old Trafford at the end of 2004 for the Grand Final between Super League giants Bradford and Leeds, I got a very clear essence of the feelgood factor that surrounds Rugby League these days.

The sport and its clubs are being wooed by blue chip companies eager to invest cash into the game. Viewing figures on terrestrial and satellite television are excellent and the myth that it is just a 'northern' or 'M62' game is a lazy myth perpetuated by journalists who have probably never attended a fixture in their lives.

The game has a strong presence in London, and not just with the Super League side of the Broncos. There is another professional club lower down the leagues, whilst the schools side of the sport is quietly flourishing in the capital. The 2004 Tri-Nations series was all about top quality international games in sold-out stadiums.

Overseas, the sport is huge in Australia and New Zealand, but how many non-Rugby League devotees are aware that the game is also popular in Fiji, Papua New Guinea, Samoa and France? It is also taking more than just a foothold in countries as diverse as Lebanon, Russia and the United States.

In this country, the standard of the game at all levels has never been higher. This is part of the reason why Rugby League is one of the best attended sports in the United Kingdom. Crowds have recently gone through the roof. The game is in very good health.

It's not just the standard of play that attracts so many supporters to regularly attend Rugby League matches, though. It is the fact that Rugby League is an affordable, safe and enjoyable family night out. Home fans stand alongside opposition supporters in modern stadia with no hint of trouble. The atmosphere is good and friendly banter abounds before, during and after the game. It truly is a family game.

Moreover, non-sport-related entertainment is put on for children, with singers and the like taking the pitch before the game and at half-time. The Rugby League community is a tight-knit one, but a welcoming one, and you can't get many better nights out than attending a fixture. If you've bought this book and never been to a Rugby League match before, do yourself a favour and go to a live match.

It may seem strange that I say that when you consider the subject matter of this book. What you are about to read, whether some people like it or not (and we'll come to that in a minute), is a factual account; a historical, factual account. The dark days contained in this book have long since disappeared. Rugby League has a fantastic record for safety at its venues and arrests are more than just a rarity. Trouble just doesn't happen these days. Police often praise Rugby League supporters after Challenge Cup finals, saying that despite the number of people there, when compared to a soccer crowd, the behaviour is exemplary. Walking to games these days is a pleasure - do not let the accounts of violence contained in this book put you off Rugby League.

The main story of this book, as you will read, takes place in the late seventies and early eighties. This book is published in 2005; times and people have changed.

So, having said all that, why did I write this book? Simple. What is contained in this book actually happened. It is a truthful and accurate account of real-life incidents. This is not a Rugby League book; it is not about the sport itself. Talking about what used to happen will certainly provoke discussion, and if that can help prevent people from getting complacent and stop such incidents from happening again, then that's what we all want.

I say again, these incidents occurred. Four months before the publication of this book, internet messageboards were abuzz about *The Family Game*. There were claims that it was based on myth; this was even before even anyone had laid eyes on the finished manuscript! Another fan pointed out: 'If it had been researched using different accounts of incidents that happened, it might have been more credible.' A valid viewpoint... if the book had even been read by this particular fan! As I hope you will appreciate, alongside the central character and the story of his experiences, there are accounts from people who support different clubs and have different viewpoints. It's not just a one-eyed account of what went on.

Of course, thousands of Rugby League fans may look at the cover of the book and scratch their heads saying, 'I've been going to games for years and never seen any trouble.' I am genuinely happy that is the case. However, it doesn't change the fact that some people did see such incidents, and it only truly hits home how frightening these situations can be if you have actually experienced them. Of course, I am not claiming that Rugby League ever had a serious hooligan problem. However, it did have hooligan elements around the edges of the sport who were intent on causing and being involved in violence in and around Rugby League venues.

You still may not believe that these things happened but, sadly, they did. Someone far wiser than myself once said: 'If you ignore history, you are doomed to repeat it.' If this book isn't your cup of tea, that's fine, I can understand your viewpoint. My own personal viewpoint is that burying your head in the sand about something that was actually a problem, albeit years ago, won't accomplish a great deal.

For every person shaking their heads at the very concept of this book, I am sure there are people nodding their heads and saying, 'Yes, that's what it was like at times.'

I remember driving home one Sunday afternoon and putting on the radio to find out the result the Challenge Cup semi-final between Hull and Leeds. Instead, I heard about Hull 'fans' invading the pitch at the McAlpine Stadium in Huddersfield. I got home to switch on *Grandstand* to see blokes on the field taunting the Leeds fans, arguing with police and tearing down the goalposts. Leeds fans remained in their section of the stadium as some Hull supporters appeared to be goading them from the pitch. Mounted police officers and dog-handlers had to be employed to clear the pitch in front of live BBC television cameras. West Yorkshire Police said fourteen people had been charged with public order offences, including nine adults and two juveniles from Hull, and a further two adults and one juvenile from Leeds. The Rugby Football League's Sir Rodney Walker said at the time that the 'sternest' action would be taken against those responsible.

He said: 'It is a great shame because the game was played in a tremendous spirit and there was no problem on the pitch between the players, then this sort of thing happens.

'We have had two tremendous semi-finals and I had hoped that I would never ever see this on a rugby league pitch.

'Make no mistake, we will deal with this with all the authority and power at our disposal.'

He went on to add: 'You only have to look around at the genuine Rugby League supporters, who are utterly disgusted with what we have seen. For their sake, we have to deal with this.' Hull would later be fined £50,000, of which £30,000 was suspended. They acted against the pitch invaders, stating that apparently fifty-two of them actually reached the other end of the field. Of those there were twenty or so who were not arrested or identified from video, but twenty-seven others who were banned. Further to that, supporters of the club signed a Fans' Charter promising acceptable behaviour. They also appointed an away fans' liaison officer, a positive move as over the years many letters have been printed in the Rugby League trade press over away fans feeling intimidated when attending games at Hull.

The incident took place on the 26th March, 2000, and it has to be the most widely publicised occurrence of Rugby League hooliganism ever. We gave Hull FC the opportunity to talk about what steps they have taken since that day and offered them space in the book to put across their views. They chose not to take up the opportunity.

The uproar this book will no doubt cause, and indeed has already caused, is a clear reflection of how passionate and dedicated Rugby League supporters are to their game. They care deeply about the image of their game. They fear that this book may be seized upon by the Union-dominated media and used as a stick with which to beat the sport publicly. That can't be the case. Rugby League is all about positivity these days and this is a story that, in the main, goes back at least twenty years.

Nevertheless, it is a story that I felt needed telling. It is a social, factual and historical account; it is not and was never intended to be a book attacking Rugby League.

Introduction

ON FRIDAY THE 26th of March, 2004 I was sat in Aussie Stadium, Sydney, Australia watching the Sydney Roosters play Canterbury Bulldogs in the National Rugby League competition whilst on a four-week holiday. That evening I saw some of the worst crowd violence ever inside a Rugby League venue. It was the lead story on the television news that weekend and made the front and back pages of the newspapers. Strangely enough, four years previously to the day, British Rugby League had seen some of its worst trouble when a group of Hull fans invaded the McAlpine Stadium pitch after a Challenge Cup semi-final.

Witnessing the shocking scenes first-hand in Australia made me think back to a feature I had spotted on a website back in 2000. It was a series of interviews conducted with a St Helens man who had been involved in off-the-field violence at Rugby League games in the seventies and eighties.

Discussing the crowd scenes that night with other internet users, I sent them the link to these accounts and was amazed by the response the material got. They all found the first-hand accounts fascinating. I managed to track down the owner of the website and asked if he had any more material from the same source. He explained that he had shelved the articles when the website closed down. I then asked him to pass on my details to the St Helens man featured in the article in the hope that he might contact me and I could find out the rest of the story. I wasn't sure whether he would get in touch, but thankfully he did and I began interviewing him to complete his story. I would like to thank the website owner for kindly letting me use his original material in this book.

I must state that I didn't want to do anything that would harm the image of Rugby League. It is often commented on and praised that Rugby League supporters of different clubs are able to mingle with each other before, during and after games with no hint of trouble.

However, it was put to me that these incidents from the past really did happen, shouldn't be swept under the carpet and, furthermore, that I should bring out this previously untold story into the open to be discussed, especially with the disturbing scenes at Aussie Stadium still fresh in my mind - scenes that ought to never be seen again within our sport.

Equally as important, I wanted to ensure that nobody reading this book is under the mistaken belief that I am a hooligan, or in any way condone hooliganism. I am not and I do not. The first-hand account you will read in the main portion of the book is taken from interviews with someone who was involved in the incidents described and understandably wishes to remain anonymous as he has long since changed his ways.

Just as someone who writes a book about murder is not a murderer, so writing a book about hooligans does not make me a hooligan, or an apologist for hooligans. I would like to state that I have never been involved in hooligan activity of any kind. The fact that most of the games described in the book take place in the seventies should give it away a little bit as I was born in 1979. I do not endorse or approve of any sort of off-the-field violence in Rugby League.

This is the true story of what used to happen in those dark days, why it stopped and how to make sure it cannot return. It is not a Rugby League book, it is a no-holds-barred look at off-the-field violence told in the hope that lessons have been learned. The point of this, as well as being a factual account, is to shock people and to make sure that the game doesn't descend into that abyss once more.

Whilst I was completing this book in January 2005, an incident at an amateur game in West Yorkshire came to my attention. So, as an additional warning about the perils of sweeping under the carpet actual occurrences of off-the-field violence and abuse, I have added a final, concluding chapter analysing this incident and its consequences for Rugby League.

CHAPTER ONE

The Family Game

ST HELENS IS a grey place. I'm not being funny and I'm not saying it's any worse than any other town you care to mention, but when you come off the motorway and see St Helens, it's grey and drab. Go somewhere nice on holiday and that happy feeling you have evaporates on approach to the town when you return home. That's not a dig at my home town, it's just the way it is and the way I sometimes feel about the place. I'm sure other people sometimes have a downer on the place where they grew up.

Having said that, I am proud to come from the town and if anyone from outside the town calls the place I get very defensive. Home is, as they say, where the heart is and my family and friends come from St Helens. It's people that make a place at the end of the day.

Undoubtedly the most, and some would say only, famous thing about the town is St Helens Rugby League club, who play their home games at Knowsley Road. I can remember my Dad taking me to Knowsley Road in the late sixties and early seventies but by the time I was thirteen, around the time of Sweet, T-Rex and other Glam Rock monsters, Mum and Dad would let me go with my mates. It was then that I first saw violence at RL games. Warrington were the main culprits. In those days all the Saints fans used to stand at the back of the Eddington Stand, which is opposite the clubhouse end of the ground if you have never been to Knowsley Road.

Usually there was a mob of about thirty to forty but when we played Wire, as Warrington were known due to the wire industry in the town, it would expand to a hundred or a hundred and fifty. There was lots of singing, most Saints fans used to go and see either Man U, Liverpool, Everton or Bolton. There were a couple who watched Chelsea, West Ham and Leeds. So the songs were right up to date with the football team name left out and Saints put in. It was quite funny thinking back now because most of us in the Eddington wore our football scarves to the game. So you could be standing next to somebody who had a Man U scarf on and you would have a Liverpool scarf on. It didn't matter though because you were Saints, which was the most important thing on those cold Wednesday nights or Sunday afternoons.

Wire always had one big mob. I can remember my first game against them. We were stood in the Eddington, it must have been fifty seconds to kick-off when the cry of 'Wire' went up. There must have been about three hundred of them and they came running up across the Eddington from the bottom corner near the main stand. I can remember seeing all these blokes, men they were and here was me at thirteen years old. God, did I run. I wasn't alone, the Warrington fans punched a hole in the Saints mob and the Saints fans were chased almost out of the Eddington End. In those days it was about taking their end. It happened quite a bit in football, like when a load of West Ham went into the Stretford End at Old Trafford. Scuffles would happen all the time.

To get back to the Wire incident though, the Wire fans were singing 'Wires, Wires'. The Saints fans regrouped (I must say at the age of thirteen I was only a spectator and spent most of my time at the back of the affray) and charged at Warrington. We were running down from the top of the Eddington where Sky commentators Eddie and Stevo used to have the box where they would introduce the game from, into the Wire fans as if our lives depended on saving the Eddington from the invaders from Warrington. The Wire fans broke, the Saints fans had retaken their ground, just like the battle on the Somme and other great historic clashes. You may ask, where were the police? There were a couple but in those days they had no control and if they caught you being naughty they would just give you a slap then throw you out of the ground.

The battle would consist of small scuffles in and around the ground with the police trying to throw as many people out as they could. It was easy to bunk back in though. So the lads who had been thrown out would be back within ten minutes. Half-time was nearly upon us and everybody, that's both sets of fans, would head for the bar although obviously not me at that age! The bar was under the main stand and if you were lucky somebody might leave or give you a drink of their beer, it was mad inside.

Say the gate was 4,500, there must have been 4,000 of them inside that small bar. Plastic glasses became the order of the day. Saints fans were on one side with Warrington fans on the other, with beer and plastic glasses being thrown at one another while the police tried to restore some kind of order. In the end the bar became shut for Saints-Wire and Saints-Wigan matches. I can always remember the beer being horribly flat as a pancake and either too warm or too cold. The only bad thing was that the bar was too small, you'd be trying to get out with people trying to get in and there was just no room.

So, it was back to see the game. A lot of time was spent not looking at the game but just swearing at the Wires fans. If Saints were getting beaten you would leave before the end. Actually, win or lose, you would leave before the end anyway with about ten minutes to go. This would be when I was around 16 years old. This was to try and ambush the away supporters. The police never did anything as we left en masse. Well, they might follow you to the training pitch at the front of the ground. Saints was a brilliant venue for fighting as it was vast, open spaces. You could walk round and there was only one way in across the training pitch. Plus we knew it like the back of our hand. All those streets around the ground, we knew exactly which entries to take. We would all make our way down the Rally. The Rally was where the trains used to run years ago, it went behind the main stand all the way down to where a supermarket is now on a road called Boundary Road. That's where the old houses were. The coaches parked down the side streets there. Bad move for the coaches. There was loads of ammo on the Rally and the coaches had to pass under an old bridge. It was the best place for ambushing coaches. I have seen many a brick go through the skylight windows in the roof of a coach. By the time the coaches had stopped you were on your toes and sprinting for Dorset. The police had realised it was more than just a game of rugby.

We had our own generals who would lead us through the backstreets of the Cambridge Road area, which was filled with terraced houses and back entries not entirely dissimilar to Coronation Street, to avoid the police. Then on to ambush the coaches again, near where the bingo hall is today, an area just before you get to St Helens town centre. Because all the houses from Beechams big clock in the town centre to Boundary Road were being knocked down, the coaches had no chance. It was guerrilla warfare, appearing in a half-knocked-down upstairs window, throwing your missile and then away you went. Everyone seemed to be throwing bricks and stones when I was growing up. I remember one incident where there were loads of stones on this field. There were two gangs of lads chucking this ammunition at each other for an hour and a half, it was war. In fact once there was this lad who had a sticking plaster over one corner of his glasses like Jack Duckworth. I must have been about fifty yards away, I hurled this stone and by chance it hit him in the other (unbroken glass) and smashed it.

Kids would also throw stones at the windows of passing trains. The kids may be bad today with what they get up to, but even they don't chuck bricks at each other like we used to do. There would very often be heads cut as a result of this type of anti-social behaviour, you'd probably end up in jail for it today.

Quite a lot of the Wire fans would catch the bus in town. It was great if you could find a couple of stragglers and give them a kicking. I hasten to add, you would not do this if they were people who had not turned out for the trouble. You know the score, you get caught, you get a good hiding. Not like today where they will cut you up. I remember when I was fifteen I got caught in the area where Asda is now, just before you get into the town centre properly. It was a Sunday game and me and my mate had thought all the Wire fans had gone home. No way, about ten of them came round the corner (Wire fans always wore their Wire scarves). We ran, but being chased over knocked-down houses wasn't easy. They caught my mate, he went down. I stopped, they were giving him a kicking. I went back to help him, me against ten of their lads. I got a kicking, they robbed our scarves, my Man United one, my mate's Leeds one. I was a bit upset but we dusted ourselves down and said 'Welcome to the family game'.

CHAPTER TWO

The Journey To Swinton

I CAN REMEMBER it like it was yesterday. I woke early that Saturday morning. It was a dry, fine day and it was 'Final day'. Saints were to play Warrington at Swinton's Station Road in the Premiership Final on the 28th of May 1977. I got myself dressed, denim shirt, Birmingham Bags and my Man United scarf. Polished 10-hole Doc Martens boots. I'd spent the Friday night giving them a spit and polish. Doc Martens boots were original heavy utilitarian workboots, then adopted by skinheads during the sixties. They re-appeared in the late seventies in a more refined form and subsequently became more casual wear, which was what we were really into. A lot of it came from punk. Punk was a style of dress that first emerged in the mid-seventies with teenagers and the unemployed, it was designed as a way to shock society through dress and music. Denim and Doc Martens were a big part of the look. I'd also somehow managed to save two pounds, which wasn't too bad really as I was still at school.

THE FAMILY GAME

Me and my mate had only decided to go to the game on the Friday as we wagged school. We decided over a game of bar billiards in a pub renowned at the time for serving under-age drinkers, with half a pint of bitter, that St Helens needed us. They were playing Wire and, as the song went, 'All St Helens stick together'. You could always get served in that particular pub. Generally, you'd have no chance in most pubs. You know how it is, you'd either have to rely on one of your mates being a big bastard and trying to get served for all of you or run the risk of trying yourself and getting laughed out of there.

I caught the ten past ten bus to town and got off in the College Street part of town, and got myself a Pimmie's meat and potato pie for the walk down to my mates. Pimmie's pies, as they are locally known, are a St Helens favourite which is quite ironic really considering St Helens people have always taken great joy in calling the Wiganers over being pie-eaters. Mind you, we all know that Wiganers are today known as Pie Eaters due to the General Strike of the 1920s. Apparently the Wigan area, one of the centres of the coal-mining industry at the time, was one of the first to go back to work, so they had to eat humble pie.

Me and my mate were good mates at school and we both loved Saints and football (sad when I think now, football does not compare to RL). Anyway I knocked for him and his mam let me in. She was just on her way out to work and said hello and asked how my mum was. She shouted upstairs: 'I'm going love, there's two pound on the cupboard, be good and I will see you later.' Just as she said that, my mate appeared down the stairs and said in his Mum voice, 'Now be good boys.' We both laughed, it was going to be a good day.

I had lived in town myself but Mum and Dad moved us out to Prescot as Dad started working for a company there, but I still kept in touch with all the lads from town. We decided we would have a drink in a pub that was known for opening early. I recently revisited the pub all these years later for a pint and you could hardly describe it as salubrious. It's a bit of a hole. As I walked in, all I could hear from these two fellas was 'fuck this' and 'fuck that' at the top of their voices. I don't think it had been decorated in decades.

Back to the story and as we walked around the corner, my mate noticed the door to the pub was open as usual. Ten past eleven, not bad.

The pub was a real drinkers' pub, it was ten past eleven and already the place was packed. It had probably been open from eight in the morning but then again it might not have shut from the night before. There were about five blokes in the corner playing 40s; it looked like they had been there all night. My mate came over with the beer, two pints of Boddies, beautiful, ice cold, the first of many I hoped to myself.

By twelve o' clock you could not move in the pub, it was rammed and quite a few lads had the same idea as us. We got a can as we walked down to either of two preferred pubs. One near the station seemed more likely because that's where we were going to catch the train to Swinton. BR had laid a special train on, it must have been an ex-football special because in the 70s they were always getting smashed up. I will tell you more about the train later.

As we walked towards the pub you could see the mass of bodies outside. As we got closer, you could see these were all Saints fans. Loads of 'em and not your divvy 'come on the Saints' type. This was a good crew. I felt proud to be part of it (there's nothing like supporting your own town). Everybody I had ever seen at Saints games was there and more besides. Where had all these lads come from? Funny thing was there seemed to be a lot of blokes. When I say blokes, I mean over twenty-five-year-olds - don't forget I was still at school.

The crowd outside was having a great time, it half spilled out into the road on both sides of the pub. Singing, shouting and swearing were the order of the day. There must have been about a couple of hundred pint glasses outside that pub and it seemed like most of it was going to end up in the cullet bin.

Most of the people in cars slowed down to avoid the Saints fans in the road. If it was a woman in a car you would get the usual rude comments, but as the beer started to work its magic, a couple of the lads would get their old lads out chasing the car up the road. This was whilst laughing to themselves 'come on love'. Most of it was harmless fun. There were two tossers in a car, definitely members of the Cambridge University Netball Team (think about it). They came speeding past the station giving it the Vees. I think they were Everton fans. They were met with a chorus of loud abuse. The mob settled for a minute, then at the top of the road somebody noticed the car.

The blue one, the one with the Everton fans in, surely not? Yes, they were coming back down the road for another bit of Woolyback piss-taking. Incidentally, the Scousers are the Woolybacks; it comes from the blokes loading the lambs off the ships in the docks breaking the strike at the time.

The lads in the car knew they had been seen but it was a one way street and they could not turn around. Now if somebody had given an order to throw at the same time, you still wouldn't have had as good a result as what happened. Bottles rained down on this car and over the road besides. The front window went through and that I can say was my work. All that stone throwing I mentioned earlier paid dividends. Bullseye brown bottles, bottom heavy, good for forty to fifty yards. They don't make 'em like that anymore.

Back to the car and it had smashed front headlights. It made a kaleidoscope of broken glass in the road, smashing I thought. The look of sheer terror on the lads' faces was unreal. They were in a bad situation. The car continued speeding past but those unlucky enough to be in the way were scattered like bowling pins. Over the road one lad was hit by the car's wing at the top of his leg. It sent him spinning like a top, lucky for him with the ten pints of lager he had more than likely downed he probably didn't feel a thing till the next day. The car was now at the top of the street. A few lads tried chasing the car but it sped off with great acceleration minus two headlights, one windscreen, one side window and plenty of dents and bumps. Somebody's dad might have been pissed off when he saw his pride and joy smashed up by Saints RL fans. Things like that didn't happen in RL, so 99.9% of people thought.

You could hear the police sirens from every direction and they were all heading towards the pub. The mob outside the pub had turned very aggressive, cars that were just driving past were met with a volley of abuse. The landlord of the pub had had enough, the doors slammed shut and his timing was bang on. Just as he locked the doors, two vans and two cars turned up. There must have been about seven coppers in them. The coppers stood on one side of the road, the mob of Saints fans on the other. For a couple of seconds everybody just stood still and looked at each other.

The police were here to restore order and that they would do. Over they marched, looking for known boys who they thought might be behind the trouble. Their sticks were drawn. Suddenly two coppers grabbed one lad. I couldn't see it all but there was a lot of scuffling, pushing and shoving with lots of dust flying about. I did see one police hat fly off somewhere which brought a large cheer. Four lads had been arrested, their arms were up their backs and they were stuffed into the police vans. One of the police officers stood in the middle of the road and shouted, 'If you are going to the game get over to the station now otherwise you are going to be nicked.' Now most people started to make their way over the road to the station but a few were arguing the toss, to which they were either punched or kicked by the coppers. This was fair game really as they were telling you fuck off now and get out of their faces and you won't get nicked. However, you still got the ones who wouldn't let it go which meant see you in court, all day Saturday stuck in the cells, probably only let you out at 5a.m. Sunday morning, nightmare.

The police herded the mob into the station and the mob of lads filled the car park outside the station. I think there must have been two to three hundred, there seemed to be lads everywhere. Me and my mate had bought our train tickets early in the week, forty pence to Swinton. I still have my ticket to this day. We needn't have bothered though, there was one ticket collector on but he couldn't do anything. He was shouting 'tickets tickets' but the police just wanted to get everybody onto the platform and onto the train so they just pushed everybody onto the platform. A few lads got nicked on the platform for having bottles and cans because all special trains were supposed to be dry.

The atmosphere was electric and songs were ringing out all over the station. 'We're all going to Swinton' and 'We hate Wires' were favourites of the day. A couple of trains pulled in on the other side of the platform going in the Liverpool direction. Abuse was shouted at anybody who looked with frowning faces at the Saints fans, cheers for anybody who raised a thumb. I can remember one Saints fan losing the plot and trying to run across the track to get on a train because somebody had given Saints the thumbs down.

Lucky for him, his mates held him back and he just screamed 'wanker' as the train pulled out of the station. Later in life, that same lad ended up working for the police. It just shows how time and the people you mix with can change you. One minute a hooligan, next thing one of the boys in blue. That day, the lad was St Helens pure red and white like the massed army of bodies on that platform.

If you have ever been to St Helens station you will know it's not the biggest in the world, so imagine two to three hundred lads drunk, rammed on that station with all the normal Saints fans who had also booked on the same train to Swinton. Quite a few of the older Saints fans left the station in disgust, I mean, fancy waiting with your wife or girlfriend for this train, you have not missed a game all season and there's pissed-up lads everywhere, effing and blinding like no tomorrow. Not very nice but these things happened.

One older Saints fan, who I would say was in his forties, asked one bunch of lads to cool it but the lads didn't take any notice of the bloke and threw a plastic cup full of piss at him. The bloke went mental and tried punching one of the lads. A scuffle broke out and the next thing the forty-year old fella was being escorted out of the station by the Bill. The six lads were warned by the police, but as soon as the police walked away they burst out laughing, cursing the boys in blue.

THE JOURNEY TO SWINTON

'It's here,' went up the cry from the far end of the station. I couldn't yet see the train but I could hear it. Suddenly I caught sight of it. What a shed! The blue of the train was black with dust. God knows how the driver could see through the windscreen, he tried using the wiper but the dust and muck just screeched across the windscreen. Anyway, that was his problem. My main concern was to get on this train with my mate. The train, if I remember rightly, was four carriages long. Four carriages for about four hundred people. Now I wasn't very good at school but four hundred into four, well, enough said.

What happened in the next ten minutes was carnage, bodies were pushing, shoving, punching, kicking, trying to get on this train. Don't forget there were no sliding doors, just the ones you opened with the brass handles, at least I think they were brass.

My mate and me were last, and I mean last, in carriage number two. The carriage was unbelievably full. At first we could not shut the door, the heat inside was unbearable and it stank of stale ale and piss. That's probably because the carriage was being used as a Stones. A Stones is of course a Piss Stones. I don't know if that comes from neanderthal times where maybe they put stones on the floor before they had a piss splashing all over their legs. There was nowhere to sit, everybody was stood, standing on their seats, it was like a sardine tin. One lad near us had managed to smuggle a couple of cans on the train, he opened one and warm sticky spray flew everywhere. I asked him for a drink, he looked at me then handed me the can. I drank, it was disgusting and warm, whatever it was. I passed it back to him saying 'Thanks mate'. Several people were saying 'Give us a drink of that mate', he passed it round at will.

All differences were forgotten today, there were lads from all parts of town; Sutton Heath, Sutton Park, Haydock (locally known as 'Yickers'), Hardshaw, Eccleston (traditionally a posh part of town), Parr (NOT traditionally a posh part of town), Carr Mill, Blackbrook, Windle (very upmarket for St Helens) and Fingerpost. There was the Rec Park area where they had a park with a bandstand in. On this bandstand, some lads had marked on it 'RPBB' - Rec Park Boot Boys. It had a vee in it for Saints. All the cream of St Helens united in the cause of Saints. St Helens boys we are here, as the song goes, drink your beer, drink your beer, forget the women bit.

The train started to move, me and my mate were jammed at the door but we managed to open the window and stick our heads out, unbelievable. Everybody had got on the train or had gone home, all that was left on the platform was empty cans and about three coppers. They looked relieved to see the train pull out of the station. The noise in our carriage was unreal, songs were ringing out everywhere. All different ones, all mixed up but they all made sense. As the train started moving out of the station, the people who hadn't realised that the train was moving began to cheer. Suddenly, as if somebody had conducted the whole carriage together, 'We're all going to Swinton' started to ring out with people banging the windows and stamping their feet on the floor. The other carriages joined in, it was unbelievable.

I don't know whether it was the motion of the train, or the four carriages full of mental Saints fans, but the train was rocking and it was hardly moving. As the train pulled past Rockware glass factory all you could hear was screaming, shouting and general unruly behaviour, it was great. To this day, I would like to know how many bodies were in our carriage. Believe me, it was chock-a-block. Most of the hardcore fans seemed to be in our carriage and to add to that, most of the fans were pissed out of their heads.

I was amazed at how much beer had been smuggled on, amongst the din you could see people opening cans and bottles. Large bottles of Fine Fayre cider somehow had managed to make their way onto the train. There was no mistaking the dark green bottle, red label and brown paper bag.

Somehow, two young lads had managed to climb up onto the luggage rack and lie on top as if they were baggage in transit off to some far-off destination, their arms hanging over the side, one of them holding a small can of pale ale. They must have only been about nine or ten years old.

Suddenly, everybody surged forward like a load of dominos falling. There was the sound of screeching brakes, bodies landing on top of each other. 'Who the fucking hell has done that? Dickheads!' Abuse was being shouted at no particular person, but it was clear somebody had pulled the emergency cord.

As I was right next to the window I could see what was happening. At that moment, what was happening was nothing. The train had stopped somewhere, not that I had any idea where. The next thing, I could see the two drivers come walking down the track to the second carriage. That was our carriage. They asked who had pulled the emergency cord, of course they were met with total silence apart from lads who were shouting abuse like 'Get this fucking train going'. The two drivers were exchanging words with the lads at the front of our carriage. There was plenty of pointing by the drivers. Suddenly, out of the window flew a full can of whatever and just missed one of the drivers, spraying beer everywhere. The drivers stood their ground and yet more words were exchanged. At this rate I could see the police being called and everybody being hauled off the train and that would be the end of the day out. If that sort of thing happened today they would just take the train back to the station.

In footy, it happened quite a few times. The train would be stopped, say just outside of Birmingham, you would be travelling to London to see your footy team, you would all be booted off just because the train got a little smashed up. At that rate, you could miss the match and not have enough money to do anything. Not that it mattered because usually you bunked on the train to away games. You normally took the Ordinary to whichever town or city. The Ordinary became the favourite towards the late seventies and early eighties. It was easier to get on and you could have more of a good time. Plus Persil used to give out free tickets with the washing powder for the ordinary. You would get there first thing in a morning, do a bit of shoplifting, put it back in a lock-up at the station, go and watch the game, come back to the station and then go home. However, that was football and only football.

Back to the train though, because where I was stood was right next to the door it became the urinal. Anyway, one bright spark said 'open the door'. I didn't but somebody else did. Lads who were dying for a piss dived towards the door. The funny thing was the train was stopped on a small bridge near a main road. People were just going about their daily chores while this train was not moving with all the doors open and lads continually pissing out of them. It must have looked a strange sight.

Without warning the train engines revved loudly, grey smoke drifted down the train from the front. Havoc still reigned in the four carriages though. A couple of lads had now got off the train and ventured onto the track. They were well drunk and they were having trouble keeping their feet on the large stones in and around the tracks. They were playing some kind of hopscotch on the sleepers while singing some songs about Saints and trying to drink their beer. Quite a few more lads also got onto the track but must have realised the danger rating and fumbled their way back onto the train. The two clowns on the track kept on with their games, it had now changed to throwing stones at the beer cans. God knows what would have happened had another train turned up.

Suddenly, the engines revved again, 'Shut the doors, shut the fucking doors, we are moving'. Surely not, but we were very slowly, doors which had been open were now slammed shut. The two lads on the track looked amazed to see the train moving. 'Come on, get on,' screamed their mates. The carriage in front opened its doors and the lads started to make their way over quickly. They both managed to get back on and all those who were watching the drama gave a very loud cheer.

The train picked up speed, a couple of lads near us seemed to know where they were and said 'It won't be long now, only about another ten minutes.' I didn't have a clue where I was and also the alcohol had started to work. I was well on my way to being pissed-up. The rest of the journey into Swinton was quite uneventful but still empty cans of beer were being chucked out of the carriage windows.

The train started to slow and the group of lads near us were making their plans, they said 'Right, straight off the train and into the ground.' Beer was being served inside the ground so you didn't have to worry about getting a drink. As the train slowed right down we passed the first station sign for Swinton, all the carriages again were abuzz. The train finally stopped, the doors burst open and out piled the troops. On the platform there was quite a large police presence waiting for the St Helens rabble. It was quite clear that the drivers of the train had radioed through and told the police that they had unruly cargo. As the bodies spilled out of the carriages, it was like the D-Day landing, bodies just pushing through the doors and landing on the platforms. I bet the Bill wondered how so many people had got on such a small train. To add to the battlefield effect the station banking on our side of the platform was burning so there was smoke drifting everywhere.

As we stood on the platform I saw one lad make an obscene gesture to a police officer. He was quickly dragged to the ground and arrested, there was to be no softly-softly tactics by the Manchester Police this day. We all waited till the whole mob was on the platform then all moved en masse, one unit toward the station steps. One booming voice from the middle shouted 'Sssaaaaiii-nnnttt Heeelleeenns'. That was just what the mob of Saints fans wanted to hear, we all joined in and charged up the steps towards the exit and out onto the streets of Swinton. Finally, we were there.

CHAPTER THREE

The Wire

I REACHED THE top of the steps and looked around for my mate. In the mad scramble up the steps we had got separated. I caught him in front of me with a group of about twenty lads. They were pointing, I didn't know what at, then suddenly I caught sight of a group of Wire fans. There must have been about five or six of them and they were shouting abuse at the Saints fans. I made my way over to my mate and said 'What the hell is going on?' He told me that just as they had got to the top of the station steps the Wire fans had thrown a couple of bottles at them. Give them their due, these lads looked game. The group of Saints lads had now swelled from twenty to one hundred, they were now in hunting mood and it's quite surprising that when you outnumber someone twenty to one you become a lot braver.

Now these Wire lads were game but not mental, there's a big difference. They shot inside some shop to escape the pack trailing them. Luckily for them, there was a copper outside the shop keeping his eye on things.

Within thirty seconds, two meat wagons pulled up outside the shop. Picture the scene, a hundred

Saints fans on one side of the road looking for blood, five Wire fans still inside the shop waiting for the Bill to tell them it's safe to come out and play without getting killed by the Saints mob.

The back doors of both the meat wagons opened and out piled eight coppers. They made a nice little segregation between us on one side of the road and the few Wire fans on the other. The Wire fans seemed reluctant to leave the safety of the police escort but they were being pushed down the street towards the ground. In the meantime, we walked down the street at the slowest pace imaginable, tracking the handful of Wire fans, looking for the easy kill. Suddenly a bottle was thrown from the Saints fans towards the handful of Wire lads. 'Come on' was being screamed as lads dodged the traffic to have a pop at the Wire fans.

If you have never been involved in a ruck or a scuffle, what happens is that you get a strange feeling. It's a sort of big rush with a feeling of not fear but, well I can't explain it. You have to have been involved in it to experience it, it's something you can't put down on paper. The best programme I ever saw on the subject was the BBC2 documentary series 'Hooligans'. That was really good because that was what it is like. Looking back, I wish I could have taken a camera with me now to take pictures and show people what it was really like, as it's such a hard thing to describe.

It's a massive adrenaline rush, there's nothing better than rattling someone with a good dig or legging another group of lads then afterwards someone saying to you 'I saw you give someone a good dig'. That was always really good. The best way I can describe what happens is basically, all your senses are heightened when it's about to go off, you're like a coiled spring. You see the other mob right in front of you and you know they are exactly the same. It's not like war where you are shooting someone from far away, it's very close and very personal. There'll be a stand-off, with plenty of 'Come on you fucking bastards'. There is a lull, a lot of fronting, it is up for somebody to go. I've been on the end where someone comes in from the other side and that's always a bad sign. If they are going to make the first move, usually a lot of your lads will get on their toes. That's why you'll hear a lot of 'Stay, stay, don't fucking run'. When you're up against organised lads who know each other and are game like Wigan, they'll just steam straight into you.

It's not so much numbers. If you've got thirty good lads, you could probably put them against a mob of sixty or seventy. A large percentage of the sixty or seventy will run, if someone in front of you turns and runs, chances are you will run to, it's a pack or herd mentality. That's why a lot of the time you'll have your main lads at the front, the sort of lads who will never run. That's a good thing but can work against the good lads as they are the ones who are going to get caught and can also be left in the position that they stay to turn round and see that everyone else has got on their toes. That's bad when you look round and loads have left you. If you're going to run, what's the point of being there, you're just getting in the way. There was definitely bitterness and repercussions when people got on their toes. At the end of the day, they let down the ones who had stayed. When it goes off, there's a massive roar and on occasions when it was warm you would get loads of dust being blown around, adding to the high drama.

It's not like 'The Quiet Man' either, a twenty-five minute choreographed brawl. It's not Queensberry Rules, it's frantic. I ran in once like a right tart, I tried to do a kung fu side-kick, I thought to myself, 'What am I doing?' Before I worked the answer to that question out, I got rattled in the side of the head. Don't forget though, this was the era of the Bruce Lee movies and everyone wanted in on the kung fu kick. Apart from Bruce though, if you tried it, you generally ended up on your arse. Doing a kung fu kick always left you open to looking like a twat. You probably were only six inches off the ground with your leg bent crooked.

During a scuffle, if you see someone in front of you, you give them a dig or a boot, simple as that. You can always spot when someone has been trained to fight though, they stand out. I know a lad who was involved in a scuffle in a St Helens pub once. It had gone off, there were eight of them and six of my mate's lot but one my mate's lot was a boxer. There was a set-to, it was going on all round them in the pub, reminiscent of a Wild West saloon. My mate got thrown against the bar, one of his mates was just stood there drinking his pint, the scream went out to him to 'Get involved'. My mate saw the boxer out of the corner of his eye and he was picking his punches, doing body punches and sorting it out. He knew what he was doing, that's the difference.

There's a difference between being hard and being game though. One night out there was a situation outside the train station. I was involved and smacked some lad with a yellow bin. One of my mates was on the floor with a lad knelt on top of him punching him. I came in from the side and rattled him. There was a lad out who most people would consider a hard man yet he didn't want to know at all, he bottled it and got on his toes. The game lads would probably be your heroes in a war, the first to get stuck in, so it works both ways. The hard lads would do it only if they really had to. Your hard lads tend to be your people involved in control sports. You put a martial arts guy up against me and he would kill me. A lad who is game will always stand his ground though.

Back to this day's action though and car horns were sounded as bodies ran across the main road. Traffic stopped in its tracks to avoid hitting anybody running across. Contact was first made at the side of a van. 'Come on you fucking bastards,' screamed this big bear of a person from Warrington. Three lads from Saints stood off for a split second about a yard from him, then piled in. The first Saints fan was smacked right in the side of the ear, which sent him tumbling into the white van. He didn't go down but was dazed. The second and third screamed and aimed boots and punches at the Yeti. They only caught him on the top of the thigh with a boot. The lad who had been smacked in the ear had had enough and legged it back across the road to where most of the Saints fans were.

THE WIRE

Two of the other Wires gave it legs and did a runner. The other two ran inside a shop where they were followed inside by six Saints fans. It was a small groceries place and full of OAPs doing their Saturday shop. What happened must have seemed very frightening to them, young men running about the shop everywhere.

The Saints fans were not in the shop to harm the OAPs, just the lads from Wire. One of the lads jumped over the counter and ran into the back of the shop. The woman behind the counter was shouting 'Eh, eh, where are you bloody going?' The other lad was trapped just behind the door near a rack of birthday cards. He was getting punched left, right and centre but he wouldn't go down. Eventually he did, where he was kicked several times about the head and body. His scarf was taken from around his neck and he was left bleeding on the floor.

I felt a bit sorry for the lad from Wire, he was getting a good kicking on the floor in the shop. Brown Doc Martens boots (footwear of the day) rained all over him, he had made himself into a little ball, a sort of primrose and blue one. The St Helens lads seemed intent on kicking this 'ball' as much as possible. I thought of putting a sly boot in but the thought passed. I'm yet to meet anybody who was involved in scuffling who has never had a kicking. If they say they never have, they've either never been there or they were too far away from the action. I know that I have and lads I know from Wigan and Warrington respectfully also have. Be it at football or rugby, that's just the way it was.

The old bloke in the shop raised his walking stick trying to fend off the hooligans from St Helens, doing his best to help the lad from Wire. This old bloke had probably done his bit for King and Country in some far-off land and most lads would respect that, they would not lay a finger on him. However, they would shout abuse like 'Fuck off granddad you stupid old bastard'. It seemed to work though, the lads who seconds earlier were kicking bells out of this lad made their way out of the shop in a sort of orderly fashion. Mind you, Kit Kats and Mars Bars were grabbed on the way out. I could still hear the commotion inside the shop as we sprinted across the road and mingled into the crowd.

As we made our way to the ground, I noticed that there seemed quite a few more Saints fans than Wire fans. Station Road was literally at the side of the railway. Our plan now was to try and get into the ground without paying, or at least only paying junior admission. Some grounds were easy to get into, others were a bit more tricky but usually it was just a large wall with barbed wire on top and the odd copper patrolling the inside wall. As we reached one end of the ground though we found quite a large police presence dotted along the outside wall. Me and my mate decided that a quick walk around the ground might be a good idea as neither of us fancied paying in at all.

That walk around the ground paid no dividends and it seemed that most of the St Helens lads had the same idea. They had no intentions of paying in either. There must have been about twenty of us stood together just outside the turnstiles. Two coppers came over straightaway. 'Right,' one said, 'either get in the ground or fuck off away from here now.' Me and my mate decided there and then to pay in as did about five or six of the other lads. We all made our way to the junior turnstiles. I would say some of the lads who got in the ground for junior admission, well, let's just say they were closer to thirty than thirteen.

I had never been to Station Road and now I realised why. Let's say three parts of the ground were okay but the large end, next to some kind of clubhouse which looked like a massive brick shed with no windows, was different. The terracing was made out of old railway sleepers and cinders. As we made our way past that massive brick shed you could see that most of the Saints fans were massed at that end. I don't know whether or not that end was called, surprise surprise, 'The Railway End' but you would have to ask some Swinton fan about that.

As we made our way up the cinder and railway sleeper terracing it was quite clear that this end of the ground was falling to bits. The dust that was coming up off the terracing was untrue. It was like being on top of a massive cinder pile. As we reached the top where the main Saints mob appeared to be assembling, it appeared there was something missing, the Wire fans had not yet arrived.

Then, I heard it...

It was like a large roar, you know the kind, a winning try in the last minute roar. One thing I was sure of was that it was the sound of troops heading this way. From where we stood in the ground on that hill of cinders and old bits of railway sleeper terracing you could see the whole main street, which led to the ground. What I could see was the whole street full of hooligans from Wire, screaming and shouting, looking for a ruck. The first thing I thought was 'Holy shit, we are going to get killed'.

God knows where the mob had come from. They must have been holed up in some boozer somewhere or their special train had just come in, but I couldn't see it being that because it was close to kick-off.

Anyway, they were here and here to do battle. Picture it, the Saints fans inside the ground have the high ground so tactically we were at an advantage. Somebody should have told the psychos from Warrington this. As they hit the bottom of the street, only the ground wall separated them from us, but did we give it to them at the bottom of that road. The old terracing broke up beautifully into loads of ammunition, we threw bricks, bottles, everything we could get our hands on. I remember one lad from town grabbing this half-sticking-out railway sleeper. It took him and another lad to lift it, they went running down the incline and launched it over the wall. From where I was stood you could see it take two lads out. One of them looked like he had caught the full thing face on and his face turned bright red with blood, he then hit the deck.

It was brilliant for us up there, they couldn't even get towards the turnstiles. There were so many bricks about, maybe we might not get killed after all.

THE WIRE

The teams were nearly ready to come out onto the field of play, another ten minutes or so I reckoned. The battle raged on however. Some of the lads from Wire were well gone and were trying to jump up over the wall. Bad idea. This other Saints fan had ripped his flag from his four foot brush steel and was smashing their fingers as they tried to climb over the wall.

By now the lads from Wire had clocked the fact that the bricks and bottles that had been thrown at them were now there to be thrown back from outside the ground back in. Incoming missiles now rained back on us. My mate caught a half-brick on the top of his shoulder, 'Bastards' he screamed. I also saw one lad, about twenty-years-old, with his mate trying to stop the bleeding from the middle of his head with his Saints scarf. Another thing I can remember was the dust, it was unbelievable. The tide of this battle had now swayed evenly.

Coppers from all parts of the ground seemed to make their way hastily towards this one end. This led to two things. Firstly, we couldn't throw any more missiles at the Wire lot without the chance of getting nicked. Some still tried though, this copper grabbed a lad who had just thrown an empty beer can. It was funny really because he gave it his hardest throw yet it just floated about twenty feet in front of him. The best way to throw a beer can is to stamp on it first as it will go a lot further. The copper grabbed him around the throat but as he grabbed him, he lost his balance. He went tumbling into all the cinder terracing and a big cloud of dust went up.

After a few seconds he emerged, gravel rash all down the side of his face and minus his copper's hat and arrest. Secondly, on this hill I noticed that the Wire influx of fans was getting bigger and bigger. The police had already started to make a segregation to keep the warring factions apart. Let's hope the Bill could do their job as the lads from Wire didn't look too happy. Would you be happy having bottles and bricks thrown at you?

Suddenly, there was a charge from the Wire lads and for a second I hit the deck and didn't know where I was...

It was the sheer number of Saints fans scattering everywhere that knocked me over and quite a few other fans as well. The lads from Wire had grouped at the bottom of the terracing and charged straight into us. They split our mob right in a soft spot. These young lads who were in front of us should have stood their ground or shouldn't have been there, but they didn't and it caused panic. Once one or two ran, the whole front seemed to disintegrate and chaos reigned supreme.

My mate grabbed me by my shirt shoulder and dragged me up backwards while I was trying to run backwards at the same time off the floor. I could see one lad from Saints through the dust who had not run and he was getting hammered by I would say three or four lads from Wire. His head was jerking back and forth with the force of the boots connecting with his skull. He couldn't lift his head up because he had long hair (order of the day) and one of the lads had it pulled low down, just the right height for kicking. He was getting punched all about the body. It looked like something from one of those wildlife films when a group of hyenas attack wild antelopes. I think that he was unconscious because his body was just like a rag doll's. They wouldn't let him drop though, you could hear women screaming and men shouting, after all they had come to watch a game of Rugby, not mindless violence.

All this was happening as the teams came out onto the pitch. It was surreal because parts of the ground were cheering the teams on not knowing what was going on at that end of the ground. From where they were, some could probably see the trouble but didn't know the ferocity of the violence.

As we stood at the top of the terracing we didn't know what to do. Where were our leaders? Where had all the coppers gone? You can never find one when you need one! Previously there had been plenty down this end of the ground but I think they had all gone for a brew en masse.

The lads from Wire stood there goading us 'Come on you St Helens bastards', hands beckoning us forward. The gap between us and them must have been about twenty yards, no man's land. They were creeping forward slowly. 'Stay, stay' you could hear voices shouting, 'Don't fucking run, stand your ground.' We did but believe me it was nerve-wracking. Suddenly, just to the left of us, I would say a group of about four blokes, when I say blokes I mean they were about forty-years-old, just went steaming right into the Wire lads. They were big lads and later that day I would find out they were from Bolton. I got talking to one and they were just there for the crack and were actually Bolton Reds (Man U). They probably saved St Helens' loss of face that day because as they hit the wall of Wire fans, who were surprised to say the least, the rest of us charged down screaming and shouting. It was now our turn to do the kicking.

Just as we all reached the Wire fans one put his head down to climb under the crash barrier. Well, I think it was a crash barrier but I did know his head was right in front of two lads from town. They booted his face at the same time, their boots caught him right in the bottom of his jaw, the other lad's boot caught him straight in his nose. The blood splattered all over them in a fine spray, he fell backwards. As I turned a lad from Wire punched me in the face with a can of something. My nose just bust everywhere, I put my head down and my hands to my face to see the damage. Then somebody pulled me out of the way of the ruck, for the second time that day I didn't know where I was...

As I lifted my head up and took my hands away from my face, blood poured out of my nose. I wouldn't mind but I used to get nosebleeds all the time and getting smacked in the face with a can didn't make it any better. It was time for me to get my bearings and assess what was happening. I know one thing that had happened in the mêlée, I had luckily ended up with all the Saints fans. The ruck still seemed to be going on because I could hear the roar and I could see plenty of dust coming up. I was also aware of missiles flying through the air.

THE WIRE

I was quite a way from where it was all going on, to tell you the truth I was trying to stop my nose bleeding. That's when I met the blokes from Bolton. One of them said to me, `Are you alright cock? Looks like you've had a bit of a smack.' He shouted to his mate, 'Tony, have you got any of that bog roll left?' His mate came over to me and pulled out loads of bog roll which was screwed up in his jeans pocket. I don't know why he had loads of bog roll in his pocket. The bloke wiped my face and tilted my head back then squeezed my nose. It worked, the bleeding stopped. The four blokes then started talking to me. They said, 'Don't worry we will get these Wire bastards back.'

Half-time was coming up and do you know I didn't even know the score, but I did know Saints were winning, which was good enough for me. I felt a push in the back. 'Where the hell have you been?' said my mate from town. We had got separated, when I turned round he looked quite shocked to see my face.

He said, 'I didn't know you'd been smacked, did you see it go off over there before?' 'I saw something,' I replied. He told me, 'We chased about ten right down to the front of the ground, you should have seen it, we really give it them, two of them jumped over the wall onto the pitch but they got nicked off the coppers.' I laughed but my nose was smarting. 'Come on,' my mate said, 'let's see if we can get some of this blood off your face.' We walked round behind the main stand where luckily the St John's Ambulance men were. They did a great job of cleaning up my face. I felt better, they were trying to ask me what had happened. I think they were just curious but wasn't sure if they would get the coppers. Anyway, I told them somebody had thrown something and it had hit me in the nose. I think they believed it but I'm not sure.

As we walked back to the end where we were stood in the first half my mate's dad came walking round the corner. He was with eight blokes, they were big drinkers all of them and they all had three or four cans each. 'Alright Dad,' my mate said, 'give us a can.' His Dad was just one of the boys and gave us a can between us. 'What's happened to you?' he asked. I told him and he said 'You two come with us now down this end of the ground and stay away from them Wire bastards, you will be alright with us.' When I told him what had happened I had not told him the whole story. My mate said, 'Listen Dad, we have left our other mates up there, we will have to go and get them and meet you near the floodlights.' His Dad said okay but I think he knew we were up to mischief and he let us go without a second question.

Off we went back to the terracing where there had been some dramatic changes involving the fans at that end of the ground. We left my mate's dad and went back to that end of the ground. Now when we got back, there was still loads of dust everywhere. I clearly remember my boots, my Martens were covered in a film of the stuff. The police had made a massive segregation between the Warrington and St Helens fans. I am sure a picture of this appeared in the press afterwards. The coppers were keeping us apart, it was surreal though, because there would be a line of ten police going down and then it stopped. So if you wanted a bit of a scuffle, you could just walk down and walk round. That's exactly what some lads were doing, you could see some scuffling going off. There was a lot of shouting abuse at each other. There was a copper stood in the middle and he shouted, 'The next one who throws something is...' This, of course, was the signal for loads of cans from both sides to fly over. It was just like arrows whizzing about at Agincourt.

We went down to the front, right to the wall. After the game finished, some lad got on the post, he shinned up it and stood on the crossbar. It always makes me laugh thinking back. You always seemed to have one lad at school who was ace at climbing. Generally he would be a right scruff but had the agility of a monkey. He could climb up anywhere; trees, lamp posts, bus shelters. You all know one from your school days I bet. I don't really remember a great deal else about the day as I was blathered. I was a teenager who'd had a bit too much ale and we all know that alcohol kills brain cells. What I do remember is when we came out of the ground there were loads of Warrington lads everywhere. There were a lot of major scuffles going off. I wanted to get back to the station as soon as possible as I was thinking about how I could get battered. We heard the roars that go off when bother occurs on our way to the station but weren't involved in it. We got to the station and were waiting for the train to come back in. There were loads of Wire lads stood on a bridge overlooking the station, a station that was still burning. The embankments were actually on fire. Someone had dropped a flag on the railway tracks, soft lad here jumped down on the track to get the flag. While I was doing this, I also decided to pass bricks up to the lads to hurl at the Wire lads on the bridge. My mate told me to get off the track or I would end up dead. Note that at no point in any of this do I try and excuse any of my behaviour, I've heard people say there wasn't much to do for fun in those days and that's true, but it's not a justification in my eyes.

Anyway, I got back on the platform, the train turned up. It was mental on the train, worse than the journey there, if you can believe it. You couldn't move at all in it, there were bodies everywhere and every one of them was pissed. I am not joking, the emergency cord was getting pulled every couple of yards. The doors were open as the train was moving on, it was just like the train to Calcutta. There was no trouble on the train though. We got back into town and one lad was so bladdered he had to go back to his mate's mam's house to get a coffee to try and sober up. He was the same lad that when he finally made his way home, fell asleep in a field a couple of hundred yards short of his front door.

It was always going to go off against Warrington, it's funny really because we never had a problem with Wigan in the early days when I think back. Warrington had a good following.

In the late seventies darts were all the rage after the Liverpool v Man U game in 1978, where a fan got hit by one. It was going off every week at football big time, it was a regular occurrence and didn't get reported on that much. As lads had seen this fad they probably thought they would have a bit of it for themselves personally. I saw it for myself one day on the way to Saints for a clash with Wire in 1979. I also had a pair of Lois Jeans. All the scousers started wearing them first. You'd wear it with Fred Perry and a pair of Samba. What it was, you remember those dart sets you used to get for Christmas? You would have the board then three green darts, three yellow darts, three blue and three red. They were really naff with shocking flights. This lad got talking to me on the way to the game and showed me one of these darts. He explained that he thought that if he threw a dart at someone and it stuck in them, it wasn't nearly as bad as stabbing someone. At the time, I agreed with him that it was alright. I can't believe what I or indeed he was thinking looking back. I was walking up by St Luke's church near Saints ground and there was a mob of Warrington who were around thirty yards away. There was bit of a stand-off between us and them.

A couple of coppers turned up. The lad with the dart was at the side of our mob as he didn't want to be seen throwing the dart by the coppers. He needed to be out of the way. There was a bit of shouting. He took the dart out of his pocket, he set it off, I watched and thought it would be lucky to fly anywhere. To mine and no doubt his disbelief, it took off like a rocket and instead of dipping, it went off. It hit a tree fifteen or sixteen feet in the air and stuck in it right by the church.

I remember after the game against Wire I caught up with one of the younger Saints lads who in his own words had 'had a bit of a nightmare' that day. After the game, he had been running after Wire fans between moving traffic on the road, he heard a car beeping and turned round to see his Dad in a car. Not good but his day didn't get better. He later threw a half knacker at a Warrington coach, it hit the corner between the side and back windows, bounced off and promptly smashed the windscreen of a car nearby. Said car was filled with four Wire lads who chased the lad down the street until he was battered by them. He achieved absolutely nothing for his considerable trouble that day.

ANOTHER SAINTS SUPPORTER GAVE HIS RECOLLECTIONS OF TROUBLE OFF THE FIELD IN THE LATE SEVENTIES AND EARLY EIGHTIES.

We all know that soccer violence became rife in Britain over twenty-five years ago, and there were some pretty bad incidents, with people getting darts in their heads and being stabbed. It was no surprise people turned away from soccer in droves. RL nipped in with the slogan 'Rugby League: A Man's Game For All The Family' in a bid to entice some of the former football supporters to watch our game.

While it is true Rugby League has never suffered the same problems of organised violence, the 'family' slogan did have a hollow ring when the sporadic outbreaks occurred at our matches. Ninety-nine per cent of matches were trouble-free, but you could usually guarantee bother at a cup game, particularly if it involved local rivals.

THE WIRE

The semi-final against Keighley at Huddersfield in 1976 saw every yob in West Yorkshire turn up to have a scuffle with the Saints fans. The following year our narrow first-round win at Wilderspool was marred by the attacks on Saints fans by Wire yobs. Warrington, being local rivals, became a bad game for violence for a few years. The worst case was the opening league game of the 1979 season.

They brought a mob of around fifty who had come specifically for a fight and Saints yobs, mostly skins and punks, went up to the back of the Eddington End to give it to them. Those who had gone up to watch the game soon scarpered down to the front as the yobs started kicking the living daylights out of each other, with the coppers carting them off down the back and putting in a cordon to segregate the warring sides. A Saints yob was arrested for carrying a chair leg.

The next few games saw scuffles and chasing against Bradford, Leigh and Hull KR, and later that season the cup game against Bradford was marred as town yobs set about bricking the coaches outside.

The cup run the following year in 1980/81 also saw trouble, but this time Saints yobs were trendier, being more into the New Romantic phase. There was fighting at Oldham in the quarter-finals and in the semi-finals against Hull KR. Although outnumbered in the semi-final, Saints yobs turned one end of the ground into running skirmishes. After the game they kicked all the windows out of the bus on the way back into Leeds city centre.

Twice in three seasons we were booted out of the cup by Wigan. On both occasions there was trouble, but at the second game in 1984, there was terrible violence. Pubs had all their windows smashed in and there was a constant battle at the Restaurant End for most of the game. One Saints spokesman went in the local paper the following week and said because it was a Sunday game it was probably the fault of football fans, which didn't quite seem to ring true.

The following season, for the first time, Saints yobs started following the club for away games. They used to get a coach and most of them were plastered before they got to the game. The local press carried stories about this "sinister St Helens Movement" or Town Baddies as they used to call themselves. They went to Bradford in the John Player and went through the old stand, nicking the flat caps of the older supporters in there.

They must have thought Yorkshire was full of easy targets, but they more than met their match when they went to Featherstone on the last day of the year-long miners' strike in March 1985. Given that coppers were about as welcome in Featherstone as the Pope at an Orange Lodge meeting, they used to have two blokes with dogs on leads patrolling the ground. One Saints coach turned up and then all hell broke loose. The crew of Saints yobs were at the back, mouthing off about the miners' strike. The next minute they were getting chased round the back of the stand by Fev fans, aged between sixteen and fifty. Saints came off a poor second and in the skirmishing one St Helens lad was slashed with a knife.

They should have known that Fev was not a place where you messed about. On the walls the graffiti used to say "Fev Riot Squad" and "Hull ran from Fev".

1986 was pretty much trouble-free, apart from a few Saints fans getting a bit of a beating at Bolton against Swinton. The following year during Saints run to Wembley there was trouble in the Popular Side bar at Wigan in the semi against Leigh, with fans attacking each other with bar stools. There were minor skirmishes for the rest of the decade but then thankfully, it died out.

MARK IS A WARRINGTON SUPPORTER WHO WITNESSED TROUBLE AT RUGBY LEAGUE GAMES IN THE EIGHTIES.

I started watching Warrington in 1978, the Australian tour match that Warrington won. I have to get that in don't I? I don't remember much about it to be honest. My sister started taking me to games as her boyfriend was a big fan of the sport. I can certainly remember the early troubles off the pitch at games in the early eighties. They used to take me to quite a few away games and I would say my main memory is probably going to Hull for the first time. I haven't got a problem with Hull, I have no axe to grind with them. I have been living in Yorkshire for fifteen years. I just remember being told at the ground that being there as an away supporter was potentially a dangerous thing to do. I thought, this doesn't fit in with what I've been told about Rugby League.

Going to Hull the first few times was quite an intimidating experience, maybe I'd led quite a sheltered life, I don't know. I remember the coach getting a police escort and still having bricks thrown at it on the way into the ground and on the way out. I remember thinking 'I don't recognise this, I wasn't told about this'.

I'd say in about 1983 or 1984 a group of us teenagers started going on the bus to Warrington away games to the local matches such as Wigan, Widnes and St Helens. My abiding memory was the almost tribal warfare aspect between local lads at that time when you went to these games regularly. You didn't recognise some of the people who went to these games. When I say recognise I don't mean personally, I mean they had nothing to do with Rugby League and that type of character wasn't readily seen at a Rugby League match. It was obviously local idiots. You could easily spot them as they tended to dress a certain way. Me and my friends noticed the problem more because we went to games on public transport, we didn't go by car or organised coaches. It seemed to us that most of the people who came to games to cause trouble would travel by public transport.

I remember hell at Widnes when one of their supporters actually ran onto the pitch and challenged one of the Warrington players, who gave him short shrift. The police carried this Widnes lad off covered in blood. There were a lot of police brought in from Warrington and Widnes that day trying to separate the gangs. It was madness. From the upbringing I had, there was no way I was ever involved in any bother or anything like it.

I also remember the battle of Burnden Park, the old John Player Trophy; I can vividly recall lads shouting 'United' and 'City' at each other. A lot of things were said after the game in the press which backed this up that it was soccer fans causing the bother. It wasn't Rugby League fans. Looking back on it now, it was nothing to do with Rugby League and that is not a kind of blinkered view. It was genuinely a social problem, it was something that young lads did that just happened to sometimes take place at a Rugby League venue. The local rivalry was an outlet for them, they weren't real supporters. The main problems were Leigh, Widnes, Wigan and Saints when Warrington played against them. That's obviously due to the geography, they're all not far apart and easy to get to from each other.

Certainly I can remember people being physically attacked at Hull and Hull KR. I'm talking about 1990 when Warrington got to Wembley, mind you. We played Hull KR on the way to Wembley at their place and it was chaotic. The violence on the streets was quite incredible; we had taken a lot of fans that day and it wasn't pleasant. I remember thinking 'I don't know why we bloody come here'. One thing happened to me years later, again at the Boulevard, when a Hull fan actually grabbed my scarf when Jonathan Davies scored. He pulled hard at the Wire scarf around my neck from behind, telling me to stop cheering. It wasn't a major incident but it was symptomatic of many people's experience of going to Hull and Hull KR. I remember when you used to walk in front of the Threepenny Stand and they would spit at you. I missed about ten years of Warrington's games at Hull because I felt that it just wasn't worth the hassle. It wasn't a Rugby League thing; it was just a group of people who congregated at what happened to be the biggest sporting event in the city that weekend.

When I went to University a few of us went to the Boulevard to watch Hull. I had a Warrington Rugby League sticker on the back windscreen of my car. After the game when I returned to my car, it had been scratched all the way round with a key. The police arrived and said 'Basically mate, there are scumbags in every town, unfortunately we seem to have more than our fair share of them.' Again, it's a social problem and Rugby League was no more than an outlet. It wasn't social exclusion as some of them were quite middle class, they were just angry, young lads with nothing else to do. They had a mindset that was tribal. I suppose it still happens in some sports but I've not seen it for a long, long time in Rugby League.

You put any crowd at any given event, when there are a large group of people gathered together there are going to be a few people there who want to cause bother. It's the same at pop concerts. There's always a few idiots where there are groups of people gathering.

I'm not saying my generation knows better or anything but I think Rugby League itself changed for the better. It became a better spectacle and people seemed to be determined to make sure that Rugby League didn't experience the terrible problems that soccer went through off the field. League truly is the family game. When the Hull fans ran on at the McAlpine Stadium in the televised Challenge Cup semi-final, to their credit Rugby League and the Hull club said 'This has got to stop' and did something about it. It would be easy for the sport to have said 'Oh, it's just a few degenerates, it's not our problem' but people were intelligent enough to say 'Look, this is organised, we've got to do something about it, it's a problem'.

If you think about it in specific terms of time, when the problems were happening years ago in the sport in the late seventies and early eighties, there was a lot of social unrest anyway in those years. There was the strikes, a lot of these lads left school at fifteen and worked in a manual job. My generation was a lot more privileged and affluent in terms of background. I'm not saying that poverty doesn't exist these days but the profile of a lot of people in those days was socially, culturally and economically different. That was a big factor. My generation has the advantage of being able to travel more, experience more and see other parts of the world. It gets you out of a small town mentality and certainly makes you a bit more tolerant. There is far more social mobility these days. The world has moved on and people have moved on.

The traditional Rugby League areas were hardest hit by the strikes, such as the miners' strike affecting Featherstone. Speaking of Fev, when we were both students me and my wife went there to watch a match. She hadn't been to many away games before this. We stood on the terraces at Post Office Road and this really scary family came up to us and said 'You've got our spot'. I wouldn't mind but there was only about two and a half thousand people in the ground, it wasn't like it was packed or anything. Some people just used to be so set in their ways and a bit small-minded. We moved of course!

The trouble did happen. People will be up in arms about this book but it's like someone writing a book about the miners' strike and the violence that ensued there. No-one would say 'Oh that's all in the past now, that doesn't happen anymore'. Of course it doesn't happen anymore, but it's important to learn various reasons why this stuff went on. I disagree with the theory that it's about disaffected youth, if you want to fight you can have a fight any day of the week. I think a twisted local pride possibly had something to do with it in some cases. That was an excuse though, as if you were from Warrington you couldn't really say you hated everyone from Wigan, you probably worked with a few due to the proximity of the places! A lot of it was soccer fans turning up for trouble in my opinion.

CHAPTER FOUR

The Football Influence

UNEMPLOYMENT DIDN'T have anything to do with scuffling. You would sign on and work on the side anyway. You'd have enough money to get by on. I left Central Modern school and got a trade as a plumber. I remember watching older blokes fighting; it was frightening to see because it's frightening even if you're not involved. A lot of it depends on the circles in which you mix. You tend to end up with your own type of lad. If you end up with a load of rabble, you'll get dragged into that mentality. It's the same in any society; it's the nature of the pack.

I started getting involved in bother at games around 1976. The main way of gaining acceptance when you start joining a bunch of lads is to be there. That's the main thing. You've got to turn up. If you're turning up at the match regularly when it was going to go off then your face will get known by the older boys. A lot of lads would know who was who from round town, you might see a gang of five lads from Eccleston and know one of them to say alright to. His mates would ask who you were and he would say that you were alright. If you were seen, you would be in the club.

In '76, we played Keighley at Huddersfield in the Challenge Cup semi-final. We went to the game and like with most games of the era, I was grogged up so my memory at times is a bit hazy. I was never usually totally drunk but well on my way. The Saints lads were in one end and there seemed to be loads of lads from different Yorkshire clubs there. There were little skirmishes going on outside the ground. There was a group of Yorkshire lads throwing a hell of a lot of bricks into the ground.

It's strange really, it wasn't usually all that organised. Sometimes you would get ten of you going in a minibus, or in later years going on a double-decker bus to Leigh for example. The St Helens Movement, as a group from one pub was known, used to organise a coach to games in the eighties and that's when it was really organised. This day, we just went on a coach.

One well-known St Helens lad took a bit of a slap. Some of their lads even came steaming onto one of our coaches. Because we weren't all together and had got split up, it was a bit of a mess. If you get split up, you're going to be in trouble. In loads of these skirmishes, I've been in with the main mob but I knew all the time the lads I was going with, I could depend on them one hundred per cent. No matter what happened, they wouldn't run, they would stay. You could set a Swiss clock by them. Ninety per cent of the time you would be with the main mob anyhow and you knew that a good percentage of the main mob wouldn't get on their toes. However, when push comes to shove there is also a percentage that will get on their toes, if you're going to get a kicking, you're going to go. It's like when one Saints lad got stabbed outside Knowsley Road and there were Saints lads who could have come out and helped him, there were only two lads who came out to have a go. All the rest of them stayed inside. We'll come to that story later though.

The trouble at League games was a throwback from watching football; I spent time watching North West football clubs. Man United wrecked the ground at Norwich one time and you could see it on the TV. Eventually, the news would be full of clips of pitch invasions at places like Luton Town and so on. We would see them and say, 'We'll have a bit of that this weekend, let's get some seats broke up and start skimming them.' Monkey see, monkey do. The best piece of footage I ever saw was two lads running, throwing seats at coppers, hugging each other and jumping up and down because they're so happy, they're having a cracking time, one of the best days of their lives. It was going on all the time in football. The worst culprits were Liverpool. In the Annie Road at Liverpool, they never used to have segregation. All the Liverpool lads used to stand at the back and the away fans would be dotted around. I remember one game against Middlesbrough that I was at. There was quite a few of us that would go from St Helens for the craic. The fashion thing came from lads from St Helens taking fashion from Liverpool. We saw about ten Boro lads, then whack, the Liverpool lads surged forward and got stuck into them. Proper scuffling going on. A few years later, they started segregating fans.

In 1977, I went to watch Liverpool and Man United in the Charity Shield at Wembley. I got a coach with a Liverpool fan even though I was supporting United. It was a mixed coach, half United and half Liverpool. For some reason, some people had taped pictures of the teams to the windows. Everyone took loads of beer on and was getting hammered but there weren't loads of proper lads on the coach or anything like that. We got to Watford Gap, they were splitting the coaches up so the Liverpool coaches were at one service station and the United coaches were at another. As our coach was mixed we were allowed in, no problem. It was chocker inside the service station, everyone rifled everything, everyone was on the rob. I had about five Mars Bars, Twixes and bags of crisps inside my jacket. Whilst inside the service station, by chance, I saw my United-supporting mate who I went to games with. I knew he was going to the game but didn't expect us to meet up. I asked him who he had come with and he told me they had got a coach together. He asked me who I had come with and I told him, he told me to forget about them and come to the game with him. I got on this United coach, everyone on it was from St Helens which was really good. I had left my ale on the mixed coach but there was loads of beer on the United coach and it was all getting passed round. Everyone ended up arseholed. There was actually a bit of a scuffle before we left the service station, one of the lads on it decked a Liverpool fan and then just jumped on the coach as we drove off.

We got to Wembley and parked up, it was dead sunny. I had a different ticket to where my mate was but in those days you had your ticket to get in the ground and once in could move to wherever you wanted. I went in with my mate. The game finished a goalless draw. When we left the ground and started getting onto our coach, you heard a big roar going up. I was sat on the coach and could see loads of scuffling going on between the coaches. You could hear lads banging into the side of the coach and could see them really going at each other. The car park at Wembley was always really full and it was pandemonium. There was a bus at the side of us full of Liverpool and one of our lads had a brush steel and ran onto the coach and was having a go at them. He was whacking these lads with it. One of their lads, and this is no word of a lie, pulled out a massive diver's knife. It must have been twelve inches long. I could see this through the window. There were other lads in front of him but he managed to make his way forward with this knife and try and have a go at our lad. The St Helens lad managed to back off, the driver shut the doors and then coppers came. People were being dragged off coaches and loads were getting nicked. We drove out of Wembley, got to the service station and we saw some Liverpool lads putting petrol in their van. The lads on our coach legged the lads in this van.

One memorable journey was when I went watching United somewhere down south on a Saturday in the FA Cup. We got to Watford Gap and found out the game was cancelled. Our coach braked, couldn't stop and slammed into another coach putting the whole of our front windscreen through. We had to come back the whole way from Watford Gap with no windscreen, it was freezing. We gave the driver loads of scarves to wrap round him.

In 1978, I was at the infamous Liverpool v Man U match where a Man U supporter got hit by a dart in the side of his nose. I was supporting Man U and went with my Liverpool-supporting mates. I was in the Annie Road end and it was bad, bad hatred, the worst I have ever seen. Liverpool were giving it loads to the Manchester fans throughout the match. There were big kick-offs all the way throughout, both inside and outside the ground. I saw the lad at the front being led out with a dart stuck in the side of his nose.

There was another Man U v Liverpool game where it went off big time, and that was the semi-final at Maine Road. With it being in Moss Side, there were lots of little streets around the ground. It seemed like the whole of Manchester had turned out for the game. Liverpool seemed to have a quarter of the Kippax and all the rest just seemed to be Manchester. Me and a mate met a lad there who had thumbed it, he was walking down a motorway which he didn't know was illegal. He got picked up by some coppers who very kindly gave him a lift into Manchester. It was an all-ticket game and we had managed to get tickets. Again, there was trouble everywhere although I wasn't involved in any of it. It did go off big time though, actually it was fucking chaos. One lad got thrown through a plate glass laundry window. It was such a mad day that I honestly don't remember how I got back home. I'm not just saying I can't believe I got home okay, I honestly can't remember.

I went to Crystal Palace watching Everton and got smashed. There were two fences that came up to about shoulder height, I would say. There were coppers stood in between the fences but not all the way down them, because there was quite a big gap. There was lots of taunting going on between both sides. The next thing I know I felt this dig in my eye. At first, I thought it was someone punching me from behind. However, I saw this lad going back across the divide after giving me a sly punch. Bastard.

Man City's lads were called M.C.C.C, the Man City Cool Cats, and they were all well-dressed lads. Me, a mate and my mate's younger brother decided to travel with Man City for the game against Leeds. We got the train down to Manchester and then the bus to Maine Road. We decided to go into the seats; remember, back then most of a ground would be standing. My mate's younger brother was only a young lad but was like a young casual as he dressed the same way as his big brother. He was dressed smartly. We went into the seats and, lo and behold, as we walked in there must have been about fifty lads stood inside. I didn't even know who they were, it didn't look good. However, they didn't give us the once-over or anything like that. It turns out they were Manchester boys who must have assumed we were the same. They were all sat behind us and I was hoping Leeds didn't score as I knew my mate's younger brother supported Leeds. Of course, Leeds scored and he started to jump up but my mate saved the day, quickly grabbing him and hissing 'Get down'. The next thing, a whole lot of Leeds lads who had been sat in the seats in the far corner ran over, that was it, it was off. There were lads running between the seats aiming kicks at each other. It was a free for all. At the end of the game, there were loads of lads hanging round the tunnel having a bit of a scuffle with the coppers. The police were dragging lads out as we left the ground. There were around sixty or seventy Leeds lads still in the ground as segregation was enforced. We left at the same time as the Man City lads so they just thought we were them.

Man U v Leeds in the late seventies was another occasion where it went off. It was the time when you had to collect tokens from certain games to get a ticket for a big match. You had to have so many tokens, they would give them out at daft games like reserve games. Lads used to go just in case their side got to the final. I got the train to Leeds in '76/'77. Quite a lot of lads got on the train at Manchester obviously. Leeds station is one hell of a walk to Elland Road. As soon as we got off the train, there were Leeds lads waiting outside the station. There was a police escort with us so they couldn't get anywhere near us but it was very intimidating. There were lads everywhere. We are talking the days of scarves, most of the lads on both sides had scarves on but were still well up for it. It was a mad walk. There were bricks coming from somewhere at one point. All you could hear were shouts of 'You're going to die Man U'. I just kept my head down. I wasn't that old at the time and it wasn't a pleasant experience. It was very on top. I remember feeling really relieved when I got to the ground. Just before going in however, I saw a lad who obviously didn't have a ticket trying to climb over a fence. He slipped and fell, knackers first, onto some spikes. He was screaming his head off.

We got in the ground and it was that packed that around forty of us ended up standing on a soil embankment looking round the stand to see the game. I was more concerned about the walk back to the station to be honest. When we got out, there were coppers everywhere but still, it was going off big time. I couldn't wait to get back to the station. Finally, I made it back and thought that I was safe at last. There were quite a lot of United lads in the station. The next thing, Leeds came running in on the other side of the station. They were mad, Leeds well wanted a go and there was no Old Bill there. Some lads were on about going over the tracks to get to them. Due to this being inside the station it was echoing really loudly and believe me when I say, it was very frightening. I picked up a paper, sat on the floor and stuck my head in the paper. I just didn't want to know, this scene was really bad. I was only a teenager and these were all blokes. I got back on the train and was made up to get home.

I went to Wolves one year and it was still standing in the away end. I got hit by a coin in the head. It really hurt and bled a lot. I remember coming out of the ground, their lads were waiting outside; it's funny when I think about it. There was a mob of Man U, who have fans from all over the country. We chased Wolves down the street and four of the lads that were round me in this mob hadn't come to the game with me and yet they too were from St Helens.

I got a slap off a copper at Tottenham one year. I had a Sex Pistols badge on the lapel of my jacket, he told me to take it off. I told him I wouldn't so he gave me a dig. You may think in those days, all this travelling would cost a bomb but you could go on the coach with loads of lads and take grog with you. So it was alright, it was a good laugh on the coach, you know the type of comments you get like 'Oh your mum rang, she wanted me to tell you you're a wanker'.

Then there was Liverpool v Arsenal in the Charity Shield of 1979. I went down on a minibus with some Liverpool fans. I just used to like going for the craic no matter who was playing. I can even remember what I was wearing at the game. I was wearing a pair of Samba, a pair of Inega jeans and a grey Levi sweatshirt. There was loads of Arsenal around but it wasn't going off. We just had a few beers around the ground. Liverpool came walking up Wembley Way, it was the biggest mob of lads I have ever seen. Hundreds of them, all casuals. Liverpool were always the best-dressed lads, they robbed quality gear on their football trips to Europe. I got a pair of Kickers off a Liverpool lad, he had robbed them before they were really fashionable. They cost me a bomb but were worth it as they were one of only two or three pairs in town at that time. Nothing happened during the game, Liverpool won comfortably. I wasn't bothered by the lack of trouble, I had come to watch the football and have a bit of a laugh.

As soon as we came down the steps after the game, there was a big mob of Arsenal, around one hundred and fifty of them in total. There was probably only about thirty or forty Liverpool in the same area and Arsenal were all tooled up. They started throwing bottles straight away, we all got on our toes. We ran down the embankment and jumped over the fence onto the grass. As it was slippy, I landed on my arse or to be more technical, my coxic. I had lost the lads I was with that day, Wembley is massive and I was on my own. I was trying to find the car in the huge car park. There were some dodgy-looking Cockney characters hanging about and I thought I was going to get caned. I wasn't happy being on my own. I went back up to the top of the embankment where it had gone off before, I heard the roar and this time there were loads of Liverpool legging the Arsenal round the stadium. You could see a few of the Arsenal getting a kick up the arse. I joined the back of the Liverpool mob and luckily saw one of the lads I had come with.

I remember when St Helens Town Football Club drew Southport away in the FA Cup, we went on the bus. There was about twenty-five of us, we went in the ground and had a walk round. We left as there was nothing happening that day.

However, Southport on Bank Holidays used to be really chocker, everyone used to go, we would go for a look. You used to be hearing rumours all the time, stuff like lads from Manchester would be fighting against lads from Liverpool. It was always full of Scousers.

Blackpool was another top scuffling destination. I remember once these Scottish lads came walking towards us and I hit one after he deliberately bumped into me. We ended up scuffling with these three Jocks. Blackpool was as mad as Ken though, it was always full of mobs. There used to be me and one other lad who would always definitely go to Blackpool. You could see lads from everywhere, even as far away as Birmingham. It was growling everywhere. As there were only two of us, it wasn't too on-top. If there had been a gang of us, it would have been unbelievable. It was chaos. I remember it going off in an arcade once between lads from Manchester and lads from Bolton. There was loads of lads running through as women were throwing the ball up for those fastest horse racing games. The commentator would be describing who was in the lead as lads were flying over it steaming into one another. Then there were lads bumping into those machines where you tried to tip the 2ps into the tray. We used to have coach dos to Blackpool. You'd go out on a Friday night round town, you'd find out that there would be a coach do the next night. You would go and have a few pints round town. There was one particular pub that the coach dos would leave from. The pub had a barman with a wooden leg. It would be quite comical, as we would be sending him up and down the bar for different things. When the coach turned up the pub would empty and you'd get lads trying to sneak full pint glasses onto the coach. The coach would be chaos, the driver would tell you not to bring any drinks on. If you walked down the street the following day you would see loads of glasses on the floor outside.

I was smoking on the coach blathered one night and because girls had big hair in them days, I accidentally brushed my cig against her hair. Due to the lacquer in her hair it started smouldering. You'd be dropped off in Blackpool and by this point you'd be well on your way drink-wise. Everywhere you tried to get in would be couples only, there were quite a few of us and we were all lads. We ended up going to a pub that was full of lads. Lads who hadn't been allowed in any other pub. Then there were four birds who had been cocked more times than Davy Crockett's rifle. It was a dive this pub. It had a dance floor at the front with silver foil hanging down from the roof as if it was Christmas. One of the lads who was with us was paranoid about snakes. Unbeknownst to him, some bloke came in the pub with a massive python round his neck, one of these 'have your picture taken holding a snake' guys. Lo and behold, he came up behind this lad who was terrified of snakes as we were on the dance floor. He put it round this lad's neck who screamed, got hold of it and fucking launched it. This snake went flying through the air before skidding across the dance floor between people's dancing feet. Some lad came bouncing over shouting 'What's going on?' at my mate so I rattled him, turns out he was a Jock. It went off big time then, the bouncers got involved and we were chucked out. We had to walk round Blackpool all night because we couldn't get in anywhere.

I started going to the music all-dayers then. I was into being a bit of a rogue and I was into the music as well, I just decided I didn't need the bother any more and got more into my music.

There were loads of good places to go if you were into your music. There were different places to go on a Friday and Saturday night, one Friday night venue was the first place I listened to Northern Soul at. I had always been into soul. There was always somewhere for you to go. One local club had a fantastic jazz-funk DJ on a Sunday. He would get all the up-to-date records from a shop called 'Spinnin' in Manchester. I always used to pop in 'Spinnin' myself when shopping to pick up the odd twelve inch. It sold all jazz funk and soul imports. Going there was like going to church in a way, something you just had to do (but actually liked, not like church!). A pilgrimage if you like. Not very big but one cool shop. Before I got into football, there would be about fifteen or sixteen of us with our baggy red jeans on and brightly coloured t-shirts with belts that hung down to your thigh, whistles and everything, all heading to the club together as we were all really into the same music. There was even the time when the record *Can You Feel The Force?* came out and some lads latched onto 'the force' aspect and brought lightsabers a la *Star*

Wars with them to the club. One lad who used to go to music events was Chad Jackson, the DJ, later famous for his hit *Hear the Drummer (Get Wicked)*. It was great, no-one had an attitude, it was chilled out, mellow and friendly with people wearing gear that some people wear now.

One club in Blackpool could be a bit iffy, I was in there once when some lads from Birmingham threw a smoke bomb in and robbed the till. It could be quite tribal as gangs from different towns and cities would turn up. I saw some great live PAs there though. They were all-dayers and they wouldn't serve ale, E wasn't on the agenda back then, it was more Speed. It used to be called the 'Heart of England Soul Club'. The music was great, you would see the same people you knew every week. You would go to Wigan Pier for their Tuesday jazz funk night, get in about three in the morning and get up for work at seven absolutely hammered. You'd see the same lads at these different venues and even though you didn't know them, you would let on to each other. You'd get talking to them.

I stopped going to the football as other interests took over, there was also the feeling that if I kept attending games it was only a matter of time before I ended up in serious trouble.

CHAPTER FIVE

The 1981 Cup Run

WE PLAYED HULL in the Challenge Cup at home in 1981. I'd just bought this new Diamond Lyle and Scott, it was red, black and yellow with thin white stripes, it was really smart. I thought I was the business because I didn't think anybody else had one. Lo and behold someone else did have one, never mind, it was still a smart jumper. We were supposed to be meeting in town and then going straight into the ground. There was a change of plan the night before and so we decided to meet in a pub nearer to the ground. Me and my mate went into the pub to wait for the rest of the lads to arrive. Then loads of Hull lads start coming in, all rugby fans with the shirts on.

All of a sudden, this dark-haired lad comes and sits down with us. He said 'Alright lads' and asked us if we were going to the rugby, he was sound. I'll always remember him, he had an umbrella with him and a beige jacket on. He was dressed the way we were. I remember him saying he went to Liverpool to do all his shopping and that we were dressed smart. In fact, he wanted to know where we had got our gear from. He told us that he went watching Hull and that he wished all their lads dressed the way we did. He turned round and said 'Look at them, they're all scruffs wearing rugby shirts.' St Helens, fashion-wise, was a really smart mob. This was due to the number of lads in the town who went watching football. On occasions when we turned out we did have a lot of casuals and we looked good. When we were all dressed up in jeans, Comfort trainers and Pierre Sangan, it was great. The Saints players actually wore Sangan when they went down to Wembley in 1987. A lot of St Helens lads would wear that, a little 'L' with an 'S' underneath it. It was a big St Helens thing so it was really good that the team wore it, it seemed like a respect thing. It probably wasn't, they probably got hold of it cheap or something.

There was a shop in Ashton that was great to buy clothes from. I used to get stuff cheap from Scousers who would go away to Europe on the rob following Liverpool. It was fantastic as they would bring back stuff you just couldn't get hold of in the UK. It was a good time with quality Adidas trainers, Farah slacks, dark jumpers and flicks, it was really smart. The clothes thing came to a point where you would wear really smart stuff to work. Stuff like Lacoste, that other lads would be wearing for going out on a weekend, you would wear for work because you had moved on fashion-wise and were well ahead of the rest. Your stuff would end up scruffy and ripped with holes in it because you'd be working in it. Dressing up for going to work just because you were that step in front. You were ahead of the lads wearing

Diamond Pringles because you'd already worn it. I remember going to Liverpool once and lads would be looking at me because of what I was wearing for work and was covered in mud. Mind you, we weren't the only ones into the fashion side of things. Warrington also had a strong section of lads heavily influenced by the fashion. You would have lads in Adidas Kick, Australian tennis, Trimm Trabs, cagoules and smoothie wedges. With all of these aspects the most important thing is uniform. All groups in society need a uniform to bond them to a group. Dress is the most obvious way to show you are part of something as it's an instant thing that people can see. The hooligans of the era obviously wanted power so they would take pride in having the newest and nicest stuff around at the time.

Dress is always an important part to any event. Notice how I remember quite clearly what I was wearing at certain games. Other lads would be the same as me. It is linked into the whole experience. I suppose people wanted to portray a certain image to the world.

Anyway, this Hull lad went on to tell us that they were bringing loads of lads today and that there was a special train bringing lads down. I don't know if he was winding us up with that last comment but I do know that after the game, try as we might, we weren't allowed near Shaw Street station so there was something going on there.

A few more of our lads came in the pub and the Hull lads told us again how many of their lads were coming and that there was probably going to be trouble. Even their lads with rugby shirts on were game. I had a few more beers and thought to myself that if they were bringing large numbers and it was going to go off, I was going to get tooled up. Not carrying a blade or anything, it was the time of the 'Millwall brick'. If you don't know what that is, it's a newspaper folded up on itself until it's about eight inches long, it's compressed really hard and if you rattle somebody with it, they would know about it. I had a newspaper with me but didn't want to mess around with that, I'd get ink all over my hands!

I went to the toilet in the pub. I was looking at the toilet roll holder. I flicked it out and at the end of the wooden holder were two metal pins sticking out. I felt that this was ideal for carrying with me. I got that and stuffed it up my sleeve under my sweatshirt. We decided to walk up by where they used to park the coaches. They were parked from where a supermarket further up Boundary Road is now up to Knowsley Road, there were absolutely loads of coaches. There were a few coppers about too. Some came up to us and asked us what we were up to. We said we were up to nothing and were just having a look at how many coaches Hull had brought. One copper got hold of me and said he was going to search me. He searched me, he ran his hands down my arms and I thought 'This is it' but somehow his hands missed the concealed toilet roll holder. He said if we were going to the game, we should go there now or otherwise, do one. We decided to go into the ground. Two of the lads decided to pay in, the other two lads who I was with decided to bunk in.

We walked round to the back of the Eddington and, using an old pallet turned on its side, climbed on it, over the wall and into the ground. My mate and me landed fine but the other lad went over on his ankle as he landed. 'Great,' I thought, 'if it goes off, we've got a cripple with us.'

We walked up to the top of the Eddington and it was packed, seemingly full of Hull fans. The whole ground seemed to be full of Hull fans, no matter where you looked. They were on the halfway line, everywhere. It was rammed packed full of them. The biggest turnout I have ever seen.

Even the coppers had black and white on that day. We decided to have a walk round the ground, to see what was happening and see where our boys were stood. We watched a bit of the game, then walked round towards the scoreboard end. This big, daft skinhead ran down and for no reason at all booted one of my mates in the back, that may I say is disgusting hooligan behaviour! Getting a kick for nothing, terrible, what did we ever do to deserve such an act? Ok, sarcasm over. He shouted at us 'Scousers' to have a go at him. To be fair, the lad he kicked did look like a Scouser with a big mad flick/wedge on his head, an Adidas cagoule, a pair of ATP trainers and a pair of F.U.S. jeans. F.U.S. jeans were really cool, you got them from the Jean Machine shop in Manchester. I had one pair of mustard F.U.S. cords and I absolutely loved them, they were the business. You also had F.U.S. jeans with red stitching. I spent quite a bit on clothes but lads used to swap clothes then. Most lads were robbing stuff so you'd get it cheap. Anyway, my mate turned round shocked at being kicked, as you would. He had been walking in front of me, I've gone to run at this skinhead and my other mate has grabbed me under the arm. As I've gone, my best Lyle and Scott, my prized possession, was ripped under the arm. I was gutted about that. Never mind the Hull lad, I felt like smacking my mate! The skinhead was bouncing up and down on the spot, he wasn't right, in fact he was a right pecker. He was soon joined by eight or nine others and with there only being three of us we didn't fancy it and walked on quickly.

We went across to behind the sticks at the old tunnel end. Again, there were loads of Hull lads there. Who should be amongst them but the lad we had chatted to in the pub earlier. He asked me if I was alright and I told him that my jumper had been ripped by 'one of the daft skinheads who comes from where you live'. He warned me, 'You'd better be quiet here mate, I can't do anything.' He was referring to the other Hull lads in the area who at that point were watching the game but some ears had pricked up at our accents and heads would soon start to turn. They were starting to clock the way we were dressed. The lad said, 'You'd better do one now or you're going to get killed, I can't do anything.' He was a genuine lad and was trying to look out for us which was really good.

We stood on the corner where the video screen is now. We got a few of us together, at least forty, some of our lads went home and some stayed. We left early and waited outside a pub near the ground. I don't know where the Hull lads had come from but I know they were game. There was a bit of a scuffle and I remember the Hull lad I had spoken to earlier trying to whack somebody with his umbrella. There were lots of shirts with him and I think he was a bit embarrassed by the standard of their attire. He dressed like us and stuck out a mile. I don't think Hull had lads like we did. Hull could not compare with the top mobs of St Helens, Wigan and Warrington. The coppers nicked a few people, the next thing we walked straight to town to see if there was any action by the station. Every route to the station was blocked off by police. There was sixty of us by now but no matter which street we tried to cut down we were faced with police. We were told by them, 'You've no chance lads'. In fact, I'm sure some Hull lads were given an escort back to the station. We even tried to get down onto the embankment to brick the train but it wasn't happening. Some people may think that with all this built-up aggression and adrenaline that we may have gone round town kicking off with anybody but that didn't happen. Although I do remember talking to one St Helens lad and he said you'll never believe it but one night, being out with a handful of lads, they saw a coach parked outside a nightclub. One lad off this coach told them to fuck off as they were Arsenal, they doubted the validity of his claim and legged him all the way down Bridge Street.

The next round was the quarter-final and we played Oldham away at Watersheddings. This was one game that was organised. I don't know whether it was organised the previous game or by lads in town passing the word on but we all knew it was going to go off. I'd seen stickers up in a couple of pubs in town, white stickers with the handwritten message: 'All St Helens to Oldham'. They were terrible though, there was that much condensation on the walls that they wouldn't stick. There was a coach that went to Oldham, fully booked up with fifty lads, we were gutted because we couldn't get on it. Ten of us ended up on a general coach. We got to the ground and Oldham Athletic had been playing in the morning, the buzz was that they would be turning out. We had a fair crew going, we had quite good numbers that day. The rumour round town the night before the game was that Saints would be taking one hundred and fifty to two hundred lads, which was a cracking turnout. That would be one of the best turnouts you could hope for. It's difficult to judge actual numbers though when you're in the midst of it. The only way you can get a halfway accurate guess at numbers is if you take a step back from everything.

Anyhow, we had a beer on our coach, the driver parked miles away from the ground by some sort of wasteground at the bottom of a hill. We found where the main mob were. We had a walk round the ground to see if there was any chance of bunking in. I certainly recall that there were lots of entries and terraced houses round the ground. I remember walking down one entry that actually led onto the ground, it had this really high wall with barbed wire at the top and I thought then that there was no way we were going to be able to bunk in. The terracing was above you as the ground was in a bit of a dip. We had to pay to get in, we were all stuck in this bottom corner, having a look round to see what was happening. We went in the big end and there was a bit of singing going on. I noticed there were a few St Helens lads there who went watching football. Oldham had a bit of a mob inside the ground and all the Saints lads started singing 'Stanley knives, Stanley knives' back at them waving what appeared to be actual Stanley knives at the opposing supporters, which shocked me until I got closer and saw what they were actually waving was the tinfoil from chewing gum wrappers, lolly sticks and in one case a twig. Mmmmm, very scary.

Once again, there was part-segregation inside the ground but once again, if you went for a bit of a walk down you could easily find yourself a scuffle. One lad from Oldham did exactly that, he walked down and looked up at the St Helens' lads and shouted to them 'Come on then'. He must have been mad, for a start, he was at a disadvantage being on the lower ground. About three lads went down and steamed him, they kicked rags out of him to be honest. I'm also sure that when Saints scored, a crash barrier collapsed and gave way. At the back of the ground, you could walk round and see outside the ground. You could see their mob outside the ground throwing bricks at the stand. These were being returned with interest. When we got outside, we were given a police escort to the coaches. We all piled back onto our coach. We were driving down the road and all these bricks came flying at the coach that was filled with the fifty lads. The coach stopped and they all piled off, we demanded that the driver of our coach let us off, initially he refused but we were adamant. We legged it down this road, God knows who we were chasing as the other lads' coach had been well in front of ours. For all I know, we could have been chasing a rabbit. I don't know if they caught up with anybody, I didn't hear anything to that effect.

Then there was the semi against Hull KR at Leeds. Before the game, I had a chunk of wood. I got a lad I knew to work it on a lathe for me. I sanded it down and it became a very handy bat with a piece of string through a hole at the end so I could put my hand through it and tuck it up my sleeve. It was light, balanced and everything. I showed it to my parents and told them that I was taking it to the game with me. They thought I was joking. I wasn't. They said I could not take it to the game so I left it behind. I don't know what I was thinking about at the time.

I had been out on the Friday night so I was still a bit grogged up. I ended up in town on the Saturday morning really early and waited for places to open so I could buy some more drink to try and get rid of my approaching hangover. I had a pair of Lee jeans on with a seam sown down the front, I had Adidas Comfort trainers on, the ones with two velcro straps over. You either had them or Puma Davis Cup trainers. Comfort were smart, they were really cool. I also had a sweatshirt on and a grey Lyle and Scott. Trainers and tracksuits emerged in fashion in the early eighties as leisure wear, when the trend for fitness spilled into fashion. It was the time of the body poppin' craze and you would go to a nightclub in a tracksuit, something I did myself once in St Helens wearing a red tracksuit with black stripes. We got to the station and it was absolutely full of lads. When I looked at it, I realised that there must have been two hundred and fifty, possibly even three hundred lads there. I remember one lad stood on a big advertising hoarding swigging from a can and singing something about Saints. We got on the train and there were coppers on it with us. The train had separate compartments, so it was dead posh even though the train itself was a shed. The journey went really quickly. The British Transport Police nicked a couple of lads on the way over, I didn't see what for. There was a lot of general misbehaving on the train, I can tell you that. One lad got hold of one of someone's Davis Cup trainers and started waving it about, then suddenly slung it out the window, so at least one lad went into the ground that day with only one trainer on. We were coming into Leeds station and Hull KR's train was pulling out of the station to let us in so that both sets of lads wouldn't be on the platform at the same time. This led to one of the most shocking incidents I have ever seen.

The trains were side by side, one moving in, one moving out. I remember looking out of the window seeing Hull KR fans shouting abuse and spitting through the window. One Saints lad ran into the compartment, unscrewed a light bulb, stuck his head out of the window and could obviously see one of their lads about to draw level with him. As the train passed, the Saints lad threw the light bulb at their supporters. The train then pulled away so I don't know what happened. It was really malicious, really bad hooliganism. This wasn't like someone getting a kicking, this was way out of hand. I sometimes wonder if the perpetrator ever thinks back about what he did that day. I would hope he feels really guilty about the incident. It's not something he should have been proud of. At the time, I remember other lads in the cabin were asking 'Who did that? That was a good idea', and the culprit said it was him and seemed happy with himself.

We got off on the platform and the word was 'Everybody stick together'. As soon as we tried to get out of the station, the coppers said 'no chance'. We were herded into a pen and told we were all to get on double-decker buses that were on their way. We saw Leeds boys around the station, there was about thirty of them, they weren't up for a scuffle, probably because they didn't know who we were. We were all 'casuals'. Suddenly, someone started singing 'St Helens' and loads of idiots joined in so they knew who we were then. We were shipped onto the double-deckers that took us to the ground. The buses were rammed full of lads. There was no room on them. As soon as the buses stopped outside the ground and we got off, there was a mob of the Hull KR lot, all divvies, they didn't have any 'smoothies' or 'casuals', whatever you want to call them. They were older blokes, one of them threw a full bottle of cider at the Saints lads. There were coppers everywhere so he got nicked. The rumour went though that as he was nicked he had eight or nine darts found on him which he had been planning to throw at of the Saints lads. Whilst there I met the lad I met the lad with the umbrella I had chatted to at the Hull home game. I had a chat with him. He'd gone with the Hull KR lads that day. He told me he had been arrested at St Helens after we had left him. I had seen him outside the pub near the ground with his umbrella.

Into the ground we went. It was quite easy to bunk into Headingley, you could get over the wall as it was quite low so quite a few of us didn't have to pay that day. Once inside, their lads were in one corner and the scoreboard end of the ground had wooden steps that led to the actual terracing and underneath them were loads of bricks. I remember grabbing some bricks and throwing them inside the ground at the Hull KR lads stood at the bottom. I had to stop though as there were so many coppers about. Some of the Hull KR lads came up in front of us and started goading us, they were massive, like bears in fact. Some of our smaller boys looked like gnomes in comparison. One lad was taunting the Saints lads, beckoning them forward with the shout 'Come on, fucking have a go'. A few of them obliged him and gave him a kicking. I was later told he was a boxer of decent standard. I steamed down and remember getting hold of a bloke and cracking him one in the side of the ear. As I cracked him, we were going tumbling underneath the crash barrier, halfway down the terracing, and as he went down one of the Saints lads gave him a boot in the head. This copper whacked me right on the back of the ear with one of them riot sticks, you can't imagine pain like it. I got dragged out of the way, luckily. There was one Saints lad who wasn't so lucky, two coppers nicked him and dragged him down to the wall. They had his arms up his back and told him to climb over the wall, he kept on telling them to fuck off. They kept on pushing his arms up in an attempt to get him over the wall. He turned round and requested 'Carry me over the wall'.

If you got nicked, you would have to go back to Leeds in midweek to attend court and you didn't want that. I can't remember much about the game. Twenty of us headed to the bar at half-time, and it was a really smart one. Five of these blokes were headed in the opposite direction, one of them was about six-foot-three. One lad took a run and performed a flying headbutt on him. The bloke just shook his head and said 'Now soft lad, what thi do that fer?', then carried on walking. His mates got a bit of a kick from some of the lads on their way past. There was one rumour that a lad from St Helens had attempted to put one Hull KR lad's head in the vat where they cook the onions. Whether it was true or not, I don't know.

We ended up watching the second half from the bar. We came out of the ground, their lot were game and were waiting for us at the end of the street. We walked towards them and I shouted 'Let's fucking get into these'. Just as these carefully chosen words had left my lips I was grabbed by a copper who dug his fingers into the sides of my throat. He told me I was nicked. I protested that I hadn't done anything. For some reason, I don't know why, he let me go. The coppers managed to shepherd their lads back down the street and stuck us back on the double-decker buses. We were watching the double-decker in front and at once, all the windows on it got smashed out by lads booting them from the inside. A few lads did the same on our bus, jumped off and went charging down the streets. I believe a fruit and veg shop got wrecked. Eventually, we were brought back to the station and put on the train home to St Helens. My ear was sore for a good while after. It's interesting to look at the nature of getting hurt and feeling pain. If someone grabs hold of you and hits you and you are in trouble, there is pain but I think you are more affected by the feeling of not being in control. You sometimes become a bit disconnected from it as if it is something happening to someone else. You can be getting kicked and be listening to the shouts of people around you screaming things like 'Leave him alone'. The force of being physically punched or kicked is obviously far from being a pleasant sensation but it's always worse the day after. You can be swollen, bruised and stiff. It's weird how quickly you forget about physical pain though, I suppose that's what allows women to give birth for a second time after the pain of the first. Generally, physical pain fades. There's the ego bruising thing of 'Shit, I got a kicking' but you can't let that bother you too much. Having said that, the mental side of pain is worse when you think about emotions.

The Hull KR day was a good result though. A lot of it is hard to gauge as, if you are in the thick of it, you can't really tell who has won or whatever.

THE 1981 CUP RUN

Anytime you get legged is a bad result. You discuss it afterwards and analyse why it has gone wrong. If you pick ten lads who will stand, you won't go far wrong and that's what Wigan always had. They would also be able to draw lads for bigger games. Similarly, we sometimes got Haydock lads for the bigger games and they always put together a good crew. Whoever says they have never lost is lying. It's funny when you're getting chased even though it's scary. You are laughing to yourself and it's probably a bit of a nervous reaction because you know if you get caught you are going to get kicked to bits. The thing that used to bother me was if I was going to get striped down the back with a blade. You're on unknown territory through the dark, terraced streets. A lot of times, things happen and don't even make the press.

One incident that certainly didn't make the press, and may well be urban legend, is a certain quite famous pop star of the eighties allegedly once turning up at Knowsley Road in a yellow fisherman's jacket and wellies and getting a good hiding.

**A ST HELENS SUPPORTER WHO HAS
RESEARCHED OFF-THE-FIELD VIOLENCE
SUBMITTED THE FOLLOWING REPORT
FOR INCLUSION IN THE BOOK,
INCLUDING SOME EVENTS HE
PERSONALLY WITNESSED.**

Ask most Rugby League supporters over a certain age and they will tell you the late 1970s was generally the main time when hooliganism was a regular happening at certain grounds within Rugby League. Unlike soccer hooligans, RL hooligans did not travel to away grounds in great numbers. Certain places always stick in the mind as having a welcoming committee that you knew could cause you some trouble. There was even a spread in one national paper reporting on some violent incidents off-the-field at Wakefield.

There were many other notable incidents. There was the so-called Battle of Station Road when St Helens and Warrington met in the Championship Final. There was trouble at Wallgate Station in 1972 when Wire and Wigan lads got stuck into each other. Both sides in Hull were generally considered to have a large-sized 'handy' mob of lads, though the rest of the Yorkshire clubs had little to offer in the hooligan stakes. At St Helens, when the away supporters were ensconced in their coaches, local hoodlums would open the emergency exit at the back of the coach, jump onboard and begin throwing punches.

Then there was the Lancashire Cup Final in 1978 at Central Park between Widnes and Workington. There was a group of Wigan lads waiting at the Wigan North Western station for supporters of the two finalists to arrive so they could start trouble with them. This led to outbreaks of violence in the town centre well before the game even kicked off. Behind one end of the ground, skirmishes continued throughout the duration of the match.

Another incident involved Featherstone fans running amok at the Recreation Ground during a BBC Floodlit Trophy game. The scoreboard was severely vandalised and objects were hurled into one end of the ground. There was even trouble in Cumbria at Workington's Derwent Park when a group of Hull KR lads were involved in a number of scuffles as well as making a distinct impression on the town centre. Another incident at the same venue occurred when Leeds travelled there for a Challenge Cup tie in the 1977/78 season. Fans of both clubs had to be separated by police on the popular side of the ground.

This possibly led to another incident between fans of the two clubs, this time at Headingley in 1982. Workington lads were arrested that day due to the trouble.

A lot of these incidents have only been in the knowledge of the people who were there, as thankfully for the image of the game, they didn't always attract publicity.

Perhaps the most notable incident of all was when the game made the back of all the major national newspapers following the violence at a derby match in Hull in the very early eighties, accompanied by gory pictures of a fan with blood running down his face after being hit by a brick. It was dreadful publicity for the game.

Fighting on the terraces was even seen on national television on at least one occasion. The 1985 Premiership Final proved to be Mal Meninga's last appearance for the St Helens club and after one Saints try you could clearly see Hull KR lads getting stuck into St Helens supporters.

The worst trouble at Knowsley Road itself I reckon was the Lancs Cup Final between Wires and Wigan in 85/86. There was 19,202 in the ground and Wigan won 34-8. However, a lad got stabbed in the back and the Saints club had windows and mirrors smashed. This made the local papers with a number of arrests. We always used to get a bit of bother when Wigan or Wires came to Saints but happily not anymore.

I can always remember my Gran even saying, 'Oh, you don't want to go when Saints play Wigan or Warrington because there's always trouble'. She also remembered a gang of thugs (as she would call them) getting escorted down Mulberry Avenue, one of the streets near to Knowsley Road. I can also remember when I was about nine walking down Knowsley Road with my Dad and we saw Saints fans chasing Wire fans near the North South club. Warrington always used to cause the most bother at Saints, there was always fighting at the Eddington end.

Another year Oldham played Wigan at Saints and there was a lot of fighting outside a pub near the ground. I think the reason there used to be bother in Rugby League is down to drink, but also down to the fact that Rugby League fans have more passion than fans in Rugby Union. There was also an influence from a few football lads who used to go to Rugby League.

One memory that sticks in my mind was the 84/85 Saints v Wigan Lancashire Cup Final at Central Park in front of an official attendance of 26,074, even though there seemed to be about 36,000 there. We won 26-18, oh mighty Mal. (I am of course referring to Saints' legendary Australian centre Mal Meninga who played a short season for the club that year. He was virtually unstoppable.)

The majority of Saints fans were at the tunnel end of the ground (which was then standing), and there had been a few small fights breaking out. The police made a segregation with the help of a few mounted officers. I was a teenager at the time and stood at the side of me were a group of fellas aged between thirty-five and forty. They were plastered and somehow one of them had got hold of a cherry and white Wigan flag. They ripped it off its thin bamboo pole and then one of them got his lighter out and set fire to it. This was a wonderful family image as you can no doubt imagine. You only see Iraqis burning flags nowadays, though sadly not Wigan ones. Coins were thrown at Saints fans that day.

The other incident at Wigan was the Challenge Cup semi in '87 versus Leigh. We won 14-8, Saints' winger Barrie Ledger had a stormer. There was fighting by where the coaches parked before the game between both sets of supporters. There was trouble in the bar, it was like a western with tables and chairs being thrown everywhere. I was in there and it just went off. Saints' coach Alex Murphy got soaked with ale by the Leigh fans. This story made the back page of the *Sunday People*, ah Rugby League, a family game.

I remember we got a rare away win at Hull KR one year in the eighties. I got told by an older fella that when I was walking out of the ground I shouldn't smile or look like I was happy because if I did they would know I was a Saints fan and I would get beat up!

We had Bradford away in the Regal Trophy in the 84-85 season, the game finished level and Saints' massive support of sixteen coachloads were chuffed. The St Helens Movement went to that game and were there to cause trouble. A few of them were on the pitch at the end of the game. As I was walking off the ground, a middle-aged man was selling hot dogs near the turnstiles until a gang of lads stole his trolley and then pushed it over into the middle of the road. They were also jumping on car bonnets with joy over our fantastic draw, either that or they had taken some more Bingo stuff.

I went to Oldham when I was twelve for a Challenge Cup game and I'm afraid to say I had two plain red and white scarves round my wrist. I can remember seeing trouble at the Kop end of the ground when a group of Saints fans mixed with Oldham fans. That was where the fighting started. A gate was smashed down and loads of people got in for nothing. The terracing wasn't the safest I've ever seen either. That was only my second-ever away game.

THE 1981 CUP RUN

We went to Wire in 1988 for a televised Challenge Cup game. There was a bit of bother at the Railway end of the ground. The Wire fans were put on the Snooker Club side with police segregating them. There was a picture of this in the *Manchester Evening News*.

As soon as the Smiths Happyways coaches pulled out of the club car park at St Helens to an away game the shout would go up, 'Could you take your scarves down please?' As if two coaches going into Fev on a Sunday afternoon were going on a sightseeing tour instead of a RL match. No matter where you were going you would be asked to take them down to stop them getting bricked when we got there. After the game, we used to have to wait behind and the police would escort the coach out of the town. That's how much of a family game it was.

There was once even trouble when Saints went to York. There was scuffling between both sets of fans. I saw trouble at the 'shed' end of the Thrum Hall ground where drunken Halifax fans were taunting Saints fans by calling them 'Scousers'. When I sit down and think about it, I've probably seen incidents of bother at every Rugby League ground. Hull KR, Featherstone and Leigh always had bad reputations in particular. I went to one Hull KR versus Leigh game, the trouble was that bad that it made the papers. They even had the police helicopter there.

An incident happened at Featherstone during the miners' strike. Before the game, where the houses are, came a few cans of lager from some Saints lads through the air, over the terracing onto the pitch. Words were said between gangs of opposing fans and fighting erupted. I can remember lads running behind the then standing area on the halfway line. All you could see flying in the air was bricks, planks, you name it. There was no police there, apart from a Security Guard with an Alsation that looked like Bagpuss. Things did quieten down in the end but it was probably the worst trouble I ever saw. One Saints lad got stabbed in the back that day.

Also, a few years later, we were changing ends and we were passing by where all the Fev fans used to stand on the halfway line. A lad I know, who now works in Finland, went into them and called them something less than complimentary. Needless to say, we all moved faster than Mr McFast from McFast Street. A younger relative of mine made his first trip to Fev when he was eight. At the end of the game we told him to hide his Saints shirt under his coat because there could be trouble. He must have been petrified.

Another Challenge Cup game, this time at Hull around 1991. The Saints fans were really getting behind their side when this seventeen foot seventy-six stone bald Hull fan appeared. He was the fella who was in the SS Experiment Camp, nope, not that, but The Wanderers. The Saints fans parted like the Red Sea when he walked up to them. Instead of hearing a roar of 'Come on you Saints', ninety-five per cent of the fans sounded like Aled Jones. He offered to take on all the Saints fans. In the end he was dragged away by two old women. One looked like Thora Hird, the other like the one out of the Krankies.

THE 1981 CUP RUN

I went watching other games away from Saints and in the Trans-Pennine Cup Final between Dewsbury and Leigh, there was trouble in the crowd and between supporters and the police. Police got involved when a group of Leigh fans started making offensive chants at Dewsbury supporters, leading to two arrests. When Dewsbury scored a try, some Leigh fans threw beer cans onto the pitch and at opposing supporters. Later police with dogs were sent into the crowd after a Leigh supporter let off a firework.

Featherstone Rovers threatened to ban any fan who caused trouble at their home ground following a problem involving one of their fans on a visit to Leigh where a skirmish between rival supporters broke out.

The most recent incident I saw occurred at Valley Parade versus Bradford in August 2001. A lot of decisions had gone against Saints and we lost the game. As the referee walked to the dressing rooms he received a barrage of boos from the Saints fans. Then, all of a sudden, there was a barrage of booze in plastic green bottles flying over my head, which landed on the pitch. It was a good job they were only plastic and they weren't filled with more lager, otherwise they would have made a nasty weapon. It was obvious it was kids drinking lager who threw the bottles so they must have been pissed-up. It was very silly of them to do this and not something they can be proud of. With it being a footy ground there were CCTV cameras so I wonder if any of them were caught throwing bottles on film. As we made our way out of the ground we saw some police jump out of their van and run down the street so something must have happened. I also saw stewards during the game at the other end of the ground dragging Saints fans out of there but I don't know what went on there. We went past a Saints coach that had pulled over and it had had its windows bricked, not very nice.

CHAPTER SIX

St Helens Scuffling

IN 1981 THERE were riots kicking off in Toxteth, problems with the coppers. There were people who fancied throwing bricks at the coppers and venting a bit of anger. Plus it was summer and it was warm. After all, you don't want to be hurling bricks in the rain; you don't want to be chucking bricks that are wet. I went to St Helens town centre one night and I'd heard rumours that it was going to go off round town this day. True enough, disturbances went off in St Helens that very night. There were loads of riot vans parked up by the police station in the town centre, they had obviously heard the same rumours and knew that something was going to happen. Rumour has it that you were not allowed to buy petrol from anywhere in a can that day as there were fears it would be used in Molotov cocktails.

I was thinking to myself if trouble was going to kick off, where would it most likely happen? It was typical St Helens really as it was very unorganised. There were a few hundred lads out and about that night, including loads of lads you'd see at a game on a weekend and your usual town hoolies. I thought it might happen at the bottom of Bridge Street in the town centre, although strategically that would have been a bad place. First of all, you need ammo and there were no bricks or stones there. Also, you'd be at the bottom of a hill with police coming down at you, which would have been no good. The best place would have been away from there where some old toilets were bring knocked down, meaning plenty of ammo. They were being demolished. That would have been a good place to be if it went off. As it happened, it didn't go off there. It went off outside a pub in the town centre. It was unbelievable. There was loads of lads inside this pub, we went outside the pub and there were police everywhere. One lad skimmed a newspaper hoarding at the coppers. It hit a car. All the traffic stopped in the road and there was a bit of a commotion with bottles being thrown.

Apparently, one lad in town had a mask on, the coppers came walking down to him saying, 'Who the fuck do you think you are? Geronimo?' We went running away from the pub as coppers were chasing everyone. At the top by the town hall there were another thirty or so lads hurling bricks at police vans. So there were two separate riots in two different locations. Better make that a hat-trick, I know a lad who got nicked the name night in the Thatto Heath area of St Helens in a disturbance that occurred there. Ok, four. It went off by another pub in town that night as well. There were loads of lads getting nicked; it was time for me to cut off home, so that's what I did. The story went round that all the cells in St Helens were full that night. However, the authorities always said that there weren't many arrests at all and that they contained the situation quite easily.

Then there was the Miners' Strike of 1984. One lad I knew was on strike and he asked me to come picketing with him to a local colliery. I remember it being fucking freezing with loads of coppers present. When the scabs were going in there was a big mad surge forward with things being thrown. After they'd gone, there'd be a little bit of scuffling, but then it would calm down. The Miners' Strike is part of the history of the town in my opinion and that's why I mention it here. The miners were shit on big time by the Tory government. The police made a load of money out of that, being paid triple time and so on. They would goad the lads who were picketing, telling them how much money they were making. St Helens was a big mining area. There are two mining monuments in the town today, it's a big part of the history of the town even though we have no pits here today. I did hear a story that had obviously been passed on from person to person quite a few times before it got to me, that one lad decided to go collecting for the miners. He went over to Europe to collect because they had nothing.

The Dutch miners, in particular, were supporting our miners. This lad travelled over to Holland and he got talking to a Dutch lad on the train. He explained to him what the situation was. The Dutch lad said he would like to make a donation but didn't have any money on him. The lad said 'no problem' but the Dutch lad insisted he wanted to make a donation. He gave him a big block of weed. As they got to customs, this lad started feeling a bit wary about it being discovered so decided to eat the whole thing. He got to this miners' meeting where they had done a collection of money and toys for the English miners' kids and he was due to speak to them. He got up on the podium and of course he was twatted, he was really, really stoned. He started playing with the cuddly toys saying, 'Nice and fluffy toys.' I think the foreign miners just thought he was a bit strange.

It wasn't just other towns St Helens lads had problems with, there was a lot of infighting. One such venue that scuffling was guaranteed to occur was at the Sherdley or St Helens Show. Held for a few days every summer and sometimes billed as the largest free show in Europe, it was held in the large Sherdley Park part of St Helens. During the late seventies the Sherdley Show used to play host to a big feud between Sutton Park, who were all scruffy bikers into heavy rock, and Sutton Heath, who town lads would side with. One year, forty of us went on the bus as we had heard it was going to go off. We walked round the fair. There were rumours that Sutton Park lads were there but nothing materialised, the coppers came and we ended up getting marched across the golf course. In the early days that was always happening, St Helens against St Helens. I read a statistic recently that said St Helens town centre had a high number of drunken assaults but it's always been that way, it's nothing new. I was once in St Helens town centre and saw three drunken louts attempt to start up a scooter parked outside a pub. They couldn't quite manage it so instead picked it up and threw it over a nearby wall where you could clearly hear parts of it smash. A totally mindless act - which they marked by giving each other high fives whilst celebrating both loudly and openly. You would get lads from town going to an estate in the Laffak area called Chain Lane to scuffle with nearby Blackbrook lads. Then you'd have lads from town centre taking on Chain Lane boys. It would get ridiculous as you would get lads from town going to Rainford. This was funny as Rainford is a country district and there would never be anyone there to fight with unless you were game for scrapping with an angry-looking cow.

There was also a time when St Helens was feuding with districts of Liverpool. One foggy Saturday afternoon we had heard that loads of lads from Huyton and Prescot, both areas on the outskirts of Liverpool, were coming to St Helens town centre. We had a gang of about sixty or seventy waiting this afternoon for the Liverpool mob to show up. Some apparently turned up, there was a cry of 'they're here', the St Helens lads went legging it through all the shoppers and chased the Liverpool lads down Bridge Street, one of the main streets in the town centre. I say the Liverpool lads but I wasn't entirely sure who we were chasing, we could have been chasing that rabbit again. They went running down the subway, we all followed, but for some reason when we got down there, we all turned to say to each other, 'Who the hell are we chasing?' We decided that we had run the other lads away and got a result. All I was doing was running after the bloke in front of me. There were lots of inter-feuds and factions from the different areas.

Another feud was scheduled to go off one Sunday at Taylor Park, a park in the Eccleston area of St Helens. I wasn't there but I heard different stories about what went on, I can't say whether it was true or not. Loads from town turned up and were at the bottom of the hill. The next thing, they looked up to the top and there was a solitary lad stood there dressed like one of the Baseball Furies from the *Warriors* film. Next thing, just like *Zulu*, loads of Huyton and Prescot lads apparently joined him at the top of the hill. Apparently some town lads had razor blades attached to vinyl records but most of the town lads got on their toes quite handy. The police turned up and that was that. Like I say, I've only ever heard this third-hand.

In the seventies you could also get coaches to Blackpool or Manchester on a Saturday night. You could always guarantee a scuffle. One time we were somewhere over the Wirral and locals were chucking stuff at our coach. However, all they had was shale so it wasn't impressive.

In 1982, when the football World Cup was on, the biggest flag was from St Helens. It had 'St Helens' written on it in big letters. It was about twenty foot by twenty foot. There were around fourteen St Helens lads who had gone over with it. They had slept under it on the beach. I know it was the biggest flag there as I have seen photos of it. You could see it on the telly a couple of times, it was massive.

Going away as a gang of lads was always good.
1983, the year *Club Tropicana* by Wham! - a top
record - came out, we went away and stayed in
Magaluf. As soon as we checked in, we made the
owner open the bar even though it was the early
hours of the morning. He warned us that there
were forty lads already in the hotel and only six
girls so our chances of pulling would not be good.
One lad proved him wrong first night when he
ended up copping off with some form of monkey.
The owner further told us that we should behave.
He had two hopes, Bob Hope and no hope. The
next day we got up and, lo and behold, there were
loads of Sheffield United lads there and also some
lads from Doncaster. I was playing table tennis, a
lad came over, around my height and quite
stocky. He asked where I was from and
introduced himself as a football hooligan. I
replied, 'That's nice for you.' All the lads in the
hotel were from the North and we stuck together,
as you often find with Northern lads when they
are away from home. We all went out one night
and got absolutely caned. We were obnoxious
lager louts. We were singing in the middle of the
road. I tried to rob some Swedish lad's trainers
while he was asleep after drinking aftershave; I
wanted them, simple as that. I also tried nicking
a watch off him but he woke up so I gave it back
to him, which was very good of me I thought!
Typical English hooligans abroad in those days.
What you have to understand is that in 1983 the
UK ruled Spain. That's what we thought anyway.
We had just won the Falklands War against the
Argies and we classed Spain as Argies too. It was

a xenophobic attitude of 'we own this place', not very enlightened times.

It was chaos. It was loads worse than what it is today. It wasn't all-day drinking in the UK back then so going over drinking all day in the sun was always going to be a catalyst for mayhem. It was Union Jack shorts time for a lot of lads. The American Navy had a massive aircraft carrier in at the time, we saw a lot of MPs (Military Police) and would generally call them tossers and take the piss out of them.

Throughout our time there, the hotel owner, a six-foot-ten massive bear-like bloke, had been giving us a hard time over the noise we had been making. On the last day there, I decided to give him something to complain about and put a dog in the pool followed quickly by sunbeds, chairs, tables, bottles and girls. I filled the pool up with anything I could get in there. I followed this up by getting hold of a scruffy, stray dog which I very kindly left on his balcony. He had a very hard time getting rid of it; it must have liked the sea view.

Speaking of going abroad, it is my ambition in life to be Captain Croc. That's my goal in life. Captain Croc, for those of you who don't know, is a bozo in a crocodile suit who runs the 'Groovy Gang' kids club on foreign holidays. Whilst parents get stuck into each other back in the bedroom and the teenagers get hammered at the nightclubs, the young bawling, puking monsters are dumped in the hands of the tour firm rep for a couple of hours each day. Sounds like a nightmare job? Not at all. You've just got to adapt it to suit your needs.

For example, you pick your resort carefully. You need somewhere with an abundance of pubs and clubs and staggering, drunk, young totty. Consider Ibiza, Magaluf, Benidorm and Tenerife. First things first, the poor saps who organise games for the kids aren't in costume so everyone can laugh at their embarrassment as they have to shout to a group of psychotic seven-year-olds 'Here we go loo be loo'. However, as Captain Croc, you're safely tucked into an oversized novelty green outfit. No one can see your face so you can dance around maniacally with the kids without fear of ridicule. Whilst the kids think you're smiling as they're throwing ice cream at you, you are really mouthing 'fuck off' at them whilst your face is safely hidden in your Croc mask. In fact, you can always throw in a few insulting hand gestures towards the group of adolescents taking the piss out of you on the beach. Usually, if you give such a gesture to a gang of beered-up louts you will get battered. However if you're in a ludicrous novelty animal suit everyone will laugh, cheer and clap.

The next thing you've got to sort out is the heat. If you're on some Spanish beach at midday and it's 100 degrees the last thing you want to be doing is running round like a mental patient in a furry outfit. No matter how hot you get though, do not attempt to swim. You are wearing a heavy outfit and you are in severe danger of drowning. Whilst you're splashing about and coming up for the last time, passers-by will be chuckling away and saying, 'Hey kids, look at funny Captain Croc trying to swim.' Then they will walk off laughing at your futile attempts to survive.

113

Obviously, being a person of culture, you're going to want to spend your free time sampling the local flora and fauna if both Flora and Fauna are obliging. You'll also want to drink heavily at night and who can blame you? However, next morning you're hungover but you have to be professional and don your outfit and take the kids away again. Obviously you will have to be careful not to let the kids get close to you otherwise you will soon hear shouts of 'Mum, Uncle Croc smells of whiskey'. However, no matter how heavy your night was, always make it back to someone's room. The last thing you need is to be found comatose, spread-eagled across the reception desk with a traffic cone on your head as many of your Groovy Gang will think you've died in a tragic road accident.

You will be expected to join in the obligatory games of beach football and this is where your cruel streak surfaces. If any of the little horrors go past you, you simply trip them up and sprint away laughing. No one will think that kindly, old Captain Croc would deliberately do such a thing. Don't let anyone take advantage of you. If you hear sunbathing parents say to their offspring, 'I'm not taking you to the water park but I'll bet Uncle Croc will take you.' Go over to the cheeky swine and say, 'Uncle Croc will bloody hell take your kids to the water park you lazy sod. Get off your fat arse and take 'em yourself.' Then march off swinging your tail triumphantly.

You may encounter a rival firm's mascot such as Lenny Lion and his 'Fun Club'. If a woman plays Lenny Lion, a cheeky grope will look to the kids like a friendly hug so get in there. You may talk to some intelligent children, however it is highly unlikely. If you do though, they may say, 'You're a crocodile, you like eating watervoles and drinking swamp water, would you like me to get you some?' This is where you reply, 'a burger and a pint of Stella will do, short arse.'

Also be prepared for one of the kids to act like the mad Aussie off the Discovery channel and go round shouting, 'What this crocky doesn't know is that I'm gonna stick my thumb up its butthole, that'll really piss him off.' Of course the fear of any mascot is someone trying to pull the head off for them but if you meet the right girl, it will happen in time.

Be careful where you spend your lunch breaks. It's not going to look too good if families are on their way to the beach and they spot you in an alley smoking a reefer and saying, 'Wow Crocky is like, super freaky man.' Similarly, if they're strolling to the pool you shouldn't be sighted in a porno bar frantically trying to unzip the front of your suit and attempting to damage yourself. When ending a day's shift make sure you don't take your costume off in sight of the punters as the shout of 'Dad, there's a man hanging out of that crocodile' will cause confusion and alarm. Neither should you panic if you can't instantly remove it off your body as you don't want kids to overhear you shouting, 'The bastard thing won't fucking come off the fucking bastard.'

At the end of the week it's time to say goodbye. As all the kids bid a tearful farewell to you and ask for a photo with you, blank them totally. Then insist that some of the nicer mums join you in a revolutionary end-of-holiday 'dance' that consists of them lying in a heap on the floor of your 'Croc Den' whilst you rub yourself against them like a tornado through the trees. The dance ends when your green fur has a suspicious white patch on the front.

Back to Rugby League, and I heard that there was bother between Saints and Leeds in 1978 for the Cup Final. I was told of a few scuffles at service stations along the way. I missed out on the trouble as there was no real way of organising it properly in those days, there were no mobile phones or websites about trouble. The only way you had of hearing about it beforehand was if you were round town and you knew the main lads, they would ask you if you were going to the game. That's how it was passed on, word of mouth. The lads who were your main lads were well-known main lads round town and older than I was. They had been watching football a long time and had more experience. They were at football when bother was at its height. They were well respected as a result. Sometimes, you would get Saints games and there would be nobody there, no lads, just normal supporters. I can remember a lot of times just walking round the ground, it was boring and cold. We didn't have a good team then either. With it being a winter game in those days, Saints always seemed to be cold, dark and depressing. All you could hear were shouts of 'man and ball'. Another thing about scuffling in winter, apart from the cold, was the mud. Places like the training pitch at Saints would be rock-hard in winter and your toes would be freezing. You would be thinking 'What am I doing here?' You would wonder whether the other lads would turn up and why weren't you either in the pub or in the warm at home. Loads of times we expected a good turnout and got badly let down. It can only be put down to bad organisation, people getting too grogged-up and the key one, it being too cold. Who wants to be scuffling when it's freezing? Saying that though, Wigan always turned up no matter what. We went to Halifax one year in the cup and we were on a coach full of numpties and grandmothers. We were expecting it to go off; six of us went into the stand and expected a turn out from both Saints and Halifax. No-one from Saints turned out and about fifteen Halifax lads. They didn't want to know though. We would have had it with them if they had wanted, even though it would have been six against fifteen.

Sometimes you would get bother at towns you wouldn't necessarily expect it at. One year we were away at Huddersfield. I had travelled there with a girl and a couple of mates. Being with a girl, I wasn't interested in getting involved in any bother. We went to a pub, there were about ten Huddersfield lads inside drinking. They were giving us the once over. It turned out there was a raffle in the pub, one of us had bought a ticket and oh yes, you guessed it, our number came up. We won a basket of food but would we leave Huddersfield in a fit enough state to eat it? To say the locals weren't happy that we had won was an understatement to say the least. I went to the toilets and four Leeds lads (I could tell they were Leeds United fans from the pin badges on their jumpers) came in behind me saying, 'We should cut these scousers up today.' Not really what you want to hear. Thankfully, we left the pub in one piece and even returned after the game to claim the basket!

There was the Featherstone game in the cup at Knowsley Road in 1983. We didn't actually go in the ground that day. We just hung around outside. It was a televised game that we watched in a pub near the ground. It's funny because at times in the eighties there didn't seem to be many coppers when it started getting on top, there was always plenty round outside the ground though. I can remember coming across the bridge and coppers telling us 'No chance lads, off you go'. It was too cold to hang around for long as they weren't going to budge so we headed back into the alehouse. I had heard it had gone off outside the ground at the Restaurant End of the ground where the Fev fans had congregated, but there was nothing happening outside.

At one point in 1984, a lad from Bolton who would come to watch Saints organised a double-decker bus to take lads to a couple of away matches. A few of us met in a pub and had a look round to see who was there. There weren't a lot of main lads out, the people who were there looked really young. I would say that the six of us there were the oldest. I thought that at least it was a start and if they were starting to get it organised we might be able to recruit a few new faces and get more lads interested. There were probably about sixty 'town bads' or 'town scals' on the bus and off we went to Warrington. There were a lot of lads from Eccleston on the bus, we knew them to say alright to but kept to our own little group.

Even though you were all together you would have your little groups of lads who had been going to games together for years. Even if there was a hundred of you, you wouldn't know everyone in that mob but it's surprising how many you did know. You could isolate groups as being with you because you might know one of them. Then you could spot who was Wigan, Warrington, etc. because you didn't know the lads. There were instances of St Helens lads getting stuck into other St Helens lads by mistake. There was a bit of an altercation on one occasion as a result of that.

This day, one lad got run over and another got a smack by the side of the bus. I remember the bus stopping at a service station and there was the infamous 'Mars Bar Snatch Squad' where loads of bars of chocolate were nicked. I was sat upstairs on the bus, it was like going on a school trip to Chester Zoo. I was shouting to the younger ones, 'Stop nicking stuff, get back on the bus, I want to get on the grog.'

The bus also went to the Leigh game. It was a miserable day, the place was a nightmare. We went to a pub near Hilton Park and we were expecting Leigh to turn up but they didn't, at least not in the first half. Most of the game was spent just being bored but a few of their lads turned up at half-time, which enlivened proceedings somewhat as there was the inevitable scuffle. Leigh was a depressing place. It was supposed to be a dry bus but we took bottles on and I remember the driver saying he didn't care what we did as long as neither him or the bus got wrecked. I heard the bus stopped running because not many people paid the lad who had organised the bus.

They had a charity event at Knowsley Road called 'Soap Aid'. This was a national event held in the wake of the mega successful 'Live Aid'. This was to be filled with soap stars, hence the name and was for some strange reason to be held in my fair home town. It was compered by Ricky Tomlinson, not the star that he is today. It was a national event; nonetheless, it went off inside the ground. It also featured various bands including Marillion, who played a 45-minute set. Lead singer Fish later made this comment about the day: 'More often than not these shows turn into disasters costing more money to organise than is actually raised. Marillion had more than their fair share in the 'Soap Aid' concert in St. Helens - I still wake up sweating!' Fish's memory of this being a bad gig can be due not only to economics, but also to a fight in the audience which caused a couple of minutes break during *Garden Party* while Fish, in a rather amused tone, called for careful handling. A nice gesture to the poor victims whose safety was put above the band's performance, as Fish simply called the band to stop playing, while he calmed down the masses. The song *Lavender* was later to be screened on

Channel 4's 'Soap Aid' programme, which covered the day's events. A Marillion fanzine would later claim that the trouble was down to a fight between the rugby supporters of Wigan and St Helens.

A mate of mine was actually there though and he said that the fighting was between security guards and a gang of towners, and was a running battle at the club end of the popular side. Nobody was watching from the terraces, everyone was on the pitch watching the gig. It was that visible that Fish had to break off singing - with the immortal words 'This is a concert, not a fucking battleground and will you lot go and fuck off.' Immediately the crowd turned round and started shouting 'fuck off' to the fighters!

There was supposed to be no drink, but one of the lads my mate saw downed a bottle of vodka inside. He was not fighting but simply kept saying, 'They will never bring anything good to St Helens ever again. We don't deserve it - because all we do here is fight!'

Also appearing that day were the stars of Albion Market - Helen Shapiro was appearing in it at the time and sang *Walking Back to Happiness* - Corrie, Eastenders, Emmerdale Farm and Grange Hill sang the famous Zammo drug storyline song *Just Say No*. Other incidents of note were that Tracy Corkhill from Brookie got wolf-whistled and Percy Sugden played his banjo. You couldn't make it up.

Ricky Tomlinson talked about how the North had so much charisma and bottle - and that is why the miners had stood out for a year against Maggie.

I wasn't there myself but what I can tell you is that it went off in town the night before big style. I hadn't been to the event as I had been in the pub. Town was chocker that night, there wasn't that many pubs in the town centre those days so everybody would be rammed in the pubs we did have. Someone from the Icicle Works (who had performed at the event) got thrown down the stairs by one of the bouncers in a pub in town. They used to have a piano in it that would play itself, I wanted to blow it up, that's how much it annoyed me.

We played Oldham in the 1987 John Player semi-final at Wigan and it was another game I went to with a bird. There was a bit of a segregation between the fans and the pair of us were actually stood next to the Oldham fans. I was shouting for Saints and these lads from Oldham were giving me loads. I threw a pint all over an Oldham lad. The bird I was with was quite sensible, she knew what I had done and went to the nearest police officer to say, 'All these lads are threatening my boyfriend.' The policeman told us to come and stand in the middle of the actual segregation. I played the innocent and piped up with, 'I wouldn't mind, I'm only trying to watch a game of Rugby League, I think it's terrible that I'm getting threatened.' I had the best view possible for the rest of the game. I kept on looking over at the Oldham lads and gave them a nice smile.

We played Salford at the Willows in the cup in 1988, the day Tony Burke dropped the ball and we went down to a shock loss. Saints took loads of lads. I remember coming out of the ground and there was a bit of scuffling and brick-throwing at the coaches.

We had it with Widnes in 1991 at Wigan in the Challenge Cup semi-final. About thirty of the Widnes lads had a big Jolly Roger flag with them. I decided to go to the game with my bird at the time and had tickets for the stand. I caught up with my mates after the game and remarked to one of them that the Widnes lads hadn't turned up. He told me that they had and were on their way as we spoke. About twenty Widnes lads came running underneath the Douglas Stand. I ended up walking down to get out of the ground with my bird, you could see lads hanging round growling and it was getting on top. As I walked away from the ground, I heard the roar as it went off. One of the Saints lads got slashed in the head. There were only five Saints lads under one of the floodlights and Widnes kept coming at them. The Saints lads stood their ground though and kept giving out digs and cracking Widnes up. The coppers came and gave them an escort to the station.

A RETIRED POLICE OFFICER CONTRIBUTED SOME OF HIS MEMORIES OF POLICING RUGBY LEAGUE GAMES WHERE TROUBLE OCCURRED.

It was the Lancashire Cup Final of 1989 when Warrington played Oldham at Knowsley Road. We were briefed that there were a load of Bolton Wanderers fans coming down as Oldham fans. We were told that they were going to have their faces painted red; at the time facepaint wasn't a common trait amongst Rugby League supporters. Your general Rugby League supporters would get to the ground five minutes before kick-off and go straight home afterwards so your troublemakers were easy to spot. We saw these Bolton fans and very early on, they got the idea that there wasn't enough of them. There were a lot of Warrington fans there, especially on the Eddington.

We had to form a segregation between the Warrington and Oldham fans. Thankfully, there were an awful lot of Bobbies on duty. We created a gap of about ten metres, we had all the regular police officers with the Warrington fans and all the specials with the Oldham fans. We had a line right down the terracing. The problem was every time Warrington scored they charged the Oldham fans. It was a bit of a nightmare. The red-facepainted lads didn't charge back, they decided that the best thing to do was to let the police get the hiding instead of them, which was quite smart thinking. We spent the entire game watching the Warrington fans and hoping their team didn't score. Unfortunately they scored often that day and it was hard work. They were trying to break through us to get to the Oldham lot. There were loads of people ejected from the ground that day. After the game we got sent on a job in the shopping centre in town and most of the people we had chucked out of the ground were running riot there. That day was one of the worst I've been involved in. I've been to a lot of pub and club fights but this was an incident that had the potential to involve hundreds if not thousands of people.

You are always going to get bother as lads will always want to fight. For example, a mate of mine told me that he would love to have an encounter with an alien. Intrigued by this unprompted statement I asked him why. He said, 'Well they're supposed to be a little bit smaller than your average human and they look like they've got massive heads, they'd be brilliant for punching.'

I now have visions of an alien strolling across for first contact with the human race, opening its mouth to start to say 'We come in peace' only to be knocked spark out.

The only other incident I remember is chucking the same Fev fan out two years running. I remember him because I went to grab him by his ear and he didn't have one!

MH, OLDHAM, SUBMITTED THIS ACCOUNT.

My first experience of violence at a Rugby League game would have to be the Challenge Cup Semi-Final on March 31st, 1986 when Oldham played Castleford at Central Park, Wigan. It was Oldham's first semi since 1964, there were twelve thousand at the game and I would say around seven or eight thousand were from Oldham. It was a nasty vibe all day; there had been various scuffles pre-game outside the ground, one Cas fan was gloating and got thrown over the bridge into the river. I wouldn't say it was organised, it just looked like beer-fuelled stuff to be honest. It all came to a head post-game. After the match, all the Cas fans came streaming onto the pitch from the Kop end at Central Park. All the Oldham fans from the pavilion end came on the pitch and they just started laying into each other. I reckon there was a couple of hundred at it easy, maybe more. I was watching it from the sidelines, I was only ten-years-old and was trying to stop this lad who had come with us from getting on the pitch. There were police and stewards there but this was pre-Taylor and it was different then. It went on for about five to ten minutes on the pitch. To this day people say it was Manchester United and Liverpool fans using the game as a smokescreen for a battle. After the game, some Cas lad tried to get into our car to start something, it was crazy. No one went coloured-up that day. It was probably just before they started wearing replica shirts. You had a scarf and that was it to be honest.

There was the Lancashire Cup final in 1989 against Wire at Saints. Both sets of fans were stood on the Eddington that day with the Wire fans on the 'Scaff' side and the Oldham fans on the main stand side. There was a line of coppers down the middle with coins and everything else flying between the two sets of fans. There was a fair bit of scuffling too. Then later in the season we met them in the Challenge Cup semi at Wigan. At half-time everyone was changing ends and they all met under the Douglas Stand. There was a few punches and stuff swung under there. I didn't really see it, but you could hear all the screams and the scuffling. The round before in the quarter-final at Widnes, all the Oldham coaches were bricked as well. We had it with Wire a few times. We played them in the Challenge Cup on a Monday night at home. They beat us and afterwards the Wire fans were in a big bunch going through the car park and past the social club when they got jumped by a load of Oldham fans and chased through the streets back to their coaches.

We also had a few scuffles with Featherstone as well, both home and away, nothing major though with only a maximum of ten involved each time. The biggest biff with them was when Nigel Heslop got his jaw broken by Brendan Tuuta and it was all going off on the pitch, that fired it up in the crowd and there were a couple of scuffles that day.

The other one that was really bad was a league game at Watersheddings around 1991. It was the last home game of the season, a B-Sky-B televised match against Hull. It was an evening kick-off so the Hull lads had been on the sauce. It was a nasty, nasty atmosphere all through the game, there were rumours of Hull fans carrying knives and everything. Nothing happened during the game. We beat them and it went mental afterwards on Watersheddings Street. I was watching from inside the ground and it was like World War Three, there were fists and everything flying, with about a hundred people involved. The Old Bill turned up and started nicking Hull fans, a couple of them ended up in court and got done.

I even saw it kick off at the Old Trafford Test match in 1994 between us and the bread thieves. That test lives in the memory, even my Dad says to this day it's the most evil atmosphere he has ever experienced at a Rugby League game. We were in the K Stand and there was a bit of a disagreement on the concourse at half-time between this guy and an Ocker so they started throwing a few punches.

Even in 2004, incidents can still occur. I go watching Leeds and there is a lot of bad blood between the Huddersfield Giants and Rhinos these days, but only at the Mac as they never bring any to LS6.

CHAPTER SEVEN

Wigan

I'D SAY A LOT of other St Helens lads got involved in trouble through football like myself. Mind you, it was already happening when I was a kid. It's probably always been happening and maybe only in the last thirty years or so has it been properly documented. As I mentioned earlier regarding the General Strike and the Wiganers going back to work first, there were a lot of pits in both St Helens and Wigan and I can imagine that being the cause of bother at games all the way back then. Of course, there's lots of bad feeling between Saints and Wigan generally. A national newspaper recently did a top ten of sporting rivalries and Saints v Wigan came third on the list. Not bad for two small northern towns. I recently got a Rugby League book from a library in St Helens and a chapter about Wigan had been very neatly defaced with the slogan 'pie-eating scum'! There is real animosity between the two sets of supporters, no game means as much to fans of both clubs.

1984 at home in the cup to Wigan really sticks in my mind. First of all, although they came onto the scene a little bit later than the likes of Wire and Saints, they always had the best mob in rugby. Their lads were watching Wigan Athletic all the time and would go everywhere with their football and rugby sides. They had a group of about thirty lads who all knew each other. Football was a lot more organised and these thirty lads picked up a lot from their football travels, they knew they could all depend upon each other. They had had it with anybody you might care to mention; Widnes, Salford, Hull etc. The pub we met in got wrecked. The Wigan lads tried to get in the pub but ended up throwing loads of things through the windows from outside it. When the windows went through, we were throwing pool balls back out the windows at them. One lad got hit in the mouth with a pool ball.

On another occasion at Knowsley Road, I had gone to the game with a bird and I went to the bar with her at half-time. Around twenty Wigan lads tried to push their way through the narrow doors of the bar, I nudged my lady companion out of harm's way. Punching and kicking broke out as there was around thirty Saints lads situated inside the bar. There was beer everywhere and I launched a plastic glass full of beer at one Wigan lad, completely soaking him from head to toe. The bar at Saints was a nightmare because it was so small. There was no room for scuffling in there. Wigan would always try and get in there though.

One Boxing Day, for Saints v Wigan at Wigan, twenty of us got the bus from town to go to the game. It took us ages to get there as the bus, quite literally, went all round the houses. We got there, it was freezing and there was nobody there. We just ended up walking round all game. I got talking to some United lads there. They were proper skinheads with Crombies on with the Lancashire Rose badge, jeans and Martens. They were into football more than rugby as they had a radio with them and were more interested in listening for the scores than watching the rugby. We got the bus back home, what a waste of time that was. I would have rather have gone there and got battered than simply nothing happening.

Another thing that happened a couple of times would be where a car would drive around the opposition town. One year in Wigan, it happened to me. I was in a Mini and we were driving round looking for strags. We were cruising along very slowly, just about to turn into a street, when we saw forty of their lads at the bottom of the street. They clocked us, lads in a car, and began walking quickly towards us. The driver asked us, 'Should we go?' 'YES' was the definitive answer and we got off like rapide. There was another year where I was alone and a car came past full of proper Wigan lads who all looked game. They gave me the once over and left it, they drove off. I was a bit relieved they did, to say the least.

There was one Wigan and Saints game at Knowsley Road, we decided we would get on at half-time as they used to let you in for free after forty minutes in those days. There were only four of us, we walked up and as we got round the corner of a pub near the ground there were about twenty of their lads stood on the bridge. They started to march towards us and we got on our toes and did one in the opposite direction.

The Lancashire Cup Final in 1985 was held at Central Park between St Helens and Wigan. One Saints lad got caught in the turnstiles by a group of Wigan lads and took a bit of a hiding. They ripped all his chains off. I don't know what else happened that day as it was one game I was unable to attend.

The Lancashire Cup final of 1986 took place at Knowsley Road and was between Wigan and Warrington, it was bound to go off. Guaranteed in fact. Those two clubs at Saints home ground was a dynamite combination. I met a load of Wire lads on holiday and we stayed in touch. They were really good lads, they arranged for me and my mate to meet up with them at a pub the day of the Cup Final. A mate of mine got a bus into town a few hours before kick-off. On the way, going down College Street, he was stunned to see loads of Wigan lads, at least forty of them, outside a pub on the street. They had got to St Helens early, another example of how organised they were. I don't know if they had hijacked a bus or not! The rumour was that they had got on a bus and told the driver where he was taking them, no arguments, simple as that. They certainly weren't out for their Sunday dinner. We went into a pub nearer the ground and Warrington had a massive mob assembled. They had brought two, maybe three double-decker buses full of lads. We went to the ground and there was no Wigan about, God knows where they were. I think Warrington were pissed off at the apparent no show.

The game went on and finished without major incident, we decided to have a beer in Saints' club. Still nothing happening, even though it was chocker in there. All the Warrington lads decided they had had enough and left. The next minute, these twenty to thirty Wigan lads came in and sat in the far corner overlooking the training pitch. I was with my group in another corner and in another corner was a mob of about twenty Saints. Numbers were pretty even. This lad from St Helens walked over to the mob from Wigan and there was an exchange of words. The St Helens lad came over to us and said, 'It's going to go off shortly, are you ready?' I told him I was, if it was going to go off I thought I might as well get into it. One lad from Wigan started to walk across the dance floor over to the mob of St Helens. Suddenly, a lad ran from the side and hit him over the head with a chair. That was it, it was on. It was like that Wild West saloon again. There were chairs and bottles from both sides flying over the dance floor in the middle. We were in no man's land really and had little involvement, although I did get a dig on the back of the head that really hurt.

Due to the dance floor being soaked with ale, it must have been like having a battle on a skating rink. One strange thing I saw that stuck in my mind was that one big, round table was spinning round upended on its side like a penny waiting to crash down. It kept going round and round. There was a bit of a stand-off then. Private security came and the Wigan lads went out through the emergency exit onto the training pitch.

Three Saints lads went out to follow them, I reckon they were expecting back-up from everybody else but it wasn't forthcoming. Little did they know as soon as they went out, the doors were locked behind them. They were in trouble. I could see it all through the windows of the club, the Wigan lads turned round to see the three lads. They started walking towards them, one of the Saints lads started gesturing to them, he must have known he was going to get a hiding but decided to have a go at them anyway. Three lads knocked him over, he was getting what appeared to be an excessive kicking on the floor. It later turned out both his ears had to be stitched as his lobes had been kicked off. Certainly I could see that his nose was streaming with blood. It looked bad for him, one lad even jumped on his head; by this time the lad was unconscious on the floor with the two lads who had gone out with him also getting a kicking.

An ambulance arrived and words were exchanged once the lad came round. I'm not sure what was said but the upshot was that at this point he refused treatment. By this time, the doors of the club had opened and loads of St Helens lads piled out, including myself. Some lads tried to talk the lad who had received the kicking to go in the ambulance to hospital. He refused in no uncertain terms. Just then, one of the lads spotted the Wigan boys going over the bridge. The cry went up to 'Do the bastards'.

We legged it across the training pitch, I couldn't see properly as I was towards the back of the group. I clearly heard one Wire lad though as he said to the guy who had been left alone with the Wigan mob, 'Look at your back, it's soaking in blood.' It turns out he hadn't just received a kicking but had been stabbed in the back. He must have been in bad pain (one lad I later talked to said you could see the muscle through the knife wound) but he carried on running in the hope of giving it back to the Wigan lads. We legged it round the corner, past a pub and could just see Wigan running round the nearby corner, we were very close to them. As soon as we got round the corner, it turned out some house was being renovated. There was a skip outside and the Wigan lads were now armed with bits of metal and pieces of wood. I couldn't believe it. The lad who had been stabbed, unbelievably, just ran into them and got a whack on the back with a piece of wood. He turned to run as everybody else had done. We were all on our toes. I later saw in the newspaper that the lad did eventually get hospital treatment and was alright. I bet he felt let down though as he must have thought some of us from inside the club would have come to help him. There was security locking the doors, but only two of them, and to be fair with the numbers we had we should have got out and helped him. The stabbing incident made the local press with the headline 'Battle of Knowsley Road'. Apparently, five other people were treated for head injuries.

When we played Leigh in the Challenge Cup semi in 1987 at Wigan, there was trouble in the town centre. There were two mobs of Saints that day. There was a load who met in a pub, fifty of us at least. This was unusual because everybody who was going on the train was meeting in the usual pub. We had a group of lads together. We left the pub en masse to go to another local and there were about another sixty or seventy lads there. We had a good sized mob all in. We were umming and aahing over what train to get. We got the train, but as soon as we got off, the coppers were trying to shepherd the Saints fans up the hill to the ground. A fair few of us saw this and hung back, this enabled us to sneak off to the alehouse over the road.

We went inside the pub mob-handed, there were forty or fifty of us. The rest of the lads were already headed up the hill singing 'St Helens, St Helens'. Because of the lads I was with, we never saw ourselves as generals or whatever in later years. We did our own thing even though we were with the main mob. If they wanted to be idiots and start singing 'St Helens' running down some streets, we would just head to an alehouse, be quiet and get ourselves a jug. We'd be out of the way. A lot of times you'd look at really young lads and think, 'What are you doing here?' Their tender years meant only one thing, they would get on their toes. I'm not saying all young lads would because some would stay. A lot of them were just tagging along but I suppose that's how you learn and you've got to start somewhere. I've done it myself. A lot of younger lads were really mouthy. I feel that lads aged around sixteen are very different sixteen-year-olds compared to my generation when we were that age. They've got no respect at all today. It's more like how I was when I was twenty-five. It's easy to be sixteen these days and stick a knife in somebody.

Anyway, we stayed in the pub for a bit then got to the top of the hill. Wigan were always waiting at the top of that hill. We didn't make a sound coming up to the top of the hill. We confronted Wigan, there was a bit of a scuffle and then they got on their toes. That's the best result we ever got, legging Wigan. There was a riot van going backwards and forwards round there. The riot van was even bumping into people as they were fighting, there were certainly arrests made. It was mad as there were loads of scuffles going off whilst people were trying to do their Saturday shopping. The fighting was where Ann Summers is now situated and it's funny to think where the battleground once was, is now the place where people pop in for dildos and anal beads.

It was chaos on this day. One of the Wigan lads was stood in a doorway, dead cheekily he rattled some Saints lad in the side of the head as he walked past. The Wigan lad then promptly scooted off. I'm not saying we gave it to Wigan that day but I think they were a bit shocked at the size of our mob. Maybe they thought we had all been put on the ground by the escort earlier on. The coppers got us all together and led us to the ground. Wigan headed to the town centre where there was further trouble later. Wigan town centre was always a good place for fighting, there was always plenty of room there.

Supporters never generally got caught up in bother. Having said that, the times where it really went off at somewhere like Wigan town centre, you couldn't help but get involved, it was that wild. It would be in the middle of the street with your old ladies trying to push along their trolley bags with bodies flying around everywhere. Wigan was always mad on a night out, their lads would have it with anyone. It used to be mental, particularly by the station. On one coach do, I saw a lad who was going to throw a beer barrel through a restaurant window in Wigan.

Supporters would get annoyed with those of us involved in bother because it was just general unruliness at the end of the day. It wasn't fair to them and it wasn't fair dragging the game down to that standard. It wasn't about the game and was absolutely nothing to do with the game at all. Realistically, when I went I didn't even watch the games. I'd say most of the lads who turned up wouldn't watch the game.

We got inside and there was segregation between the Saints lads and Leigh lads. Leigh surprised me with their turnout, the farmers as I called them. Even though they were all yokels, bumpkins and wurzels, they were as game as anything. They were all older blokes with rugby shirts on. They were giving us abuse. The bar was open at half-time, so we went down there; it was tiny and loads of Saints lads were in there. The next thing we knew, about ten to fifteen Leigh lads came in. They walked past us, one of them had a Leigh hat on and one lad whipped it off the back of his head. He turned round and as soon as he did so, someone else from the side of me punched him in the head. That was it then, it went off. The Leigh lads got caned inside, there were chairs and tables flying everywhere. The floor was soaking, just covered in ale. I'm sure I tried booting one of their lads up the arse but slipped and managed to knacker my foot by kicking a Saints lad in his

Achilles. It also knackered him as well. It just goes to show you that it doesn't always go to plan. Everyone thinks it's Queensberry Rules-style of fighting but it most certainly isn't, it is sheer chaos. The coppers piled in the bar and dragged people out.

We decided to get out of the ground before the end of the game, I'd say thirty of us came out and made our way back out to Wigan town centre to get the train. We were getting an escort and when we got down towards the station Wigan were there again waiting for us with one difference, they were organised this time. They let us walk past down the hill, then they came legging it down behind us. There was fighting amongst the traffic on the road, the police went ballistic. We may have got on our toes a little bit. There were a few scuffles by the station but as soon as punches were thrown, the coppers were there straight away to break things up and send us on our merry way back to St Helens and the waiting alehouse.

At Wembley that year, at the very bottom of the St Helens end, was a Halifax fan lying prone in a river of ale and piss. He'd been dusted by a group of Saints lads.

We were due to play Widnes in the 1989 Challenge Cup semi-final at Wigan. We met in a pub and we were trying to decide what time train to catch. We were actually debating whether to go or to watch the match on the pub television. I reckon there were about sixty lads inside the pub. We decided to go to the game, we got off the train and there was a heavy police presence. We couldn't even get a drink in the pub over the road.

We were told to go to the ground straight away. We got to the top of the hill and Wigan were waiting for us. There was a bit of a scuffle there, not much happened though.

We got split up into two mobs. I was in a mob of twenty and we ended up walking down a street at the back of the old picture house. The rest of the mob were taken by the police to Central Park. We were in the street, I heard a cry of 'They're here now'. Wigan were as game as anything. Here indeed they were, running down the street towards us. We spread out over the road as you do in these situations, there's usually a stand-off for a couple of seconds. One lad next to me threw a full can of Coke at a Wigan lad and it rattled him right in his chest making a not inconsiderable sound. One of their lads came steaming in, I don't know what he was thinking about; he was flailing his arms and legs like an octopus but not making any contact. He ended up against a wall and got a bit of a hiding. There was a Scouse lad with us, God knows what he was doing there. He piped up with, 'It's great this, it's better than football.' Credit to the Wigan lad, he didn't go down, we chased them back up the hill and then the coppers came to split it up. We ended up back with the main mob.

At the ground itself, trouble was caught on national television, very briefly. There was a big double gate at Wigan where fans would be let out of the Central Park ground. There were only around twenty Saints lads sat on the wall, unbeknownst to the Wigan lads there was around another ninety Saints boys on the other side of where the floodlight was. The Wigan lads came running in at the twenty on the wall but were promptly chased out. This led to an incident where a police horse stood on one unfortunate lad's foot and ripped his jeans. Widnes had a bunch of Scouse lads at the game but we didn't really have it with them properly.

It even went off with Wigan at Wembley on more than one occasion. In 1989, Saints were to play Wigan in the final. Originally, we were supposed to be going down on the Friday but ended up going down on the Saturday morning instead. Some lads did go down on the Friday and it didn't go well for them. Rumour has it that one St Helens lad got slashed in Soho although I did hear they gave Wigan a kicking on the Underground. The four of us who went on the coach that was organised by a pub felt that it would be full of grannies and so on. How wrong were we? It was a coach full of around fifty pure hooligans. There was a bin on the coach for pissing in, loads of beers and a few lads were taking Speed to keep them going after getting on the beer the night before. The coach was very smoky due to a few lads smoking blow, one fella tried to open the skylight but was told to 'Fuck off, we're trying to get stoned here'. Around ten in the morning, we stopped at a service station. I went for a piss and noticed this Wigan lad was staring at the Saints fans. As I walked out of the service station I noticed another Saints lad overtook the lad and butted him in the side of the head. Another Saints lad screamed at him to leave it out as it was too early in the day for that sort of thing.

The same lad caned someone after the game so it must have been the time of the attack and not the violence itself he was averse to.

Two years later the same two teams were back at Wembley. I'd got a new top for the occasion. We parked up at Wembley and walked under the subway. Some Wiganers came walking along in the opposition direction shouting abuse at us. One of them took a dig from one of our lot but they weren't really lads so we left it at that. We got out into the open and saw a group of about twenty Wigan fans over the road. Despite us being outnumbered one lad was in no mood to be cautious, he went running into them and punched this massive bloke. Bad move. He just got looked at, then hit, splitting his eye open and putting him on his arse in the gutter. He gathered himself together as the other Saints lads told him he really needed to calm down. Somehow, I had managed to get myself in the good seats that day, not too far from the Royal Box. I was not good company for the people who had landed out cash for top seats that day. I stood on my seat hurling abuse towards Wigan. I was simply horrible that day.

A COUPLE OF WIGAN MEN TOLD ME THEIR MEMORIES OF TROUBLE AT RUGBY LEAGUE GAMES IN DAYS GONE BY.

It wasn't organised or anything in the early seventies but there were a few Wiganers involved in bother. Most of the trouble happened with Warrington. Wigan and Warrington was the big thing. To be honest with you, at the time Wigan couldn't match Warrington. We always had a good do at them. The problem was a lot of the time, Wigan lads wouldn't go to Warrington. I remember once a group of us got on the train, got to Warrington station, walked to the ground, had a mooch about and then went back home.

Wigan is supposedly a rugby town and in those days it definitely was. I started going to games with a group of Wigan lads and rugby was where you went. There was nothing else to do. There was a lot more rugby than Latics in those days. A lot of Wigan lads would go watching Man U as well. We'd go watching Man U with Warrington lads, they would be on the same train as us and we'd be alright with each other. On the way home, the train would pull into Warrington station and as they got off they would be saying, 'We'll be seeing you tomorrow.' On Saturday we were all Man U and would have no trouble, the next day it was back to normal.

The Fletcher Street end at Warrington, the home end, you could never take that off them whereas they could come to Wigan and take our end of the ground.

I've been to Knowsley Road a few times from the seventies onwards. I've been there when there was no Wiganers bar a handful, say ten or fifteen, then I've been there when we've had hundreds of lads. I've been to Knowsley Road, kept my head down and been chased back to the station. I've left there at half-time because we've been getting battered by Saints lads. I've been to finals at St Helens, Wigan v Salford was a good one. We did St Helens outside the ground. One of the main St Helens lads at the time took a bit of a slap that day. I saw him whilst out shopping the other week. If you met Salford that day, you knew you'd met Salford. They were a bit of a handful to say the least. They were big Man U lads and very dodgy characters. We had to come back on the train with them and it was a nightmare. We got off at Wigan station, they got off with us and chased us down the street.

When Warrington or St Helens came to Wigan, the police would move their lads out of the ground and walk them through the town centre to the station. We would do one round the back of the pictures and be waiting for them at the top of the hill. It would go off where Woolies was and then be cat and mouse from there all the way to the station.

Semi-finals were some of the best ones at Central Park. You would have your Wigan lads, then whoever your semi-finalists were, whether it be Warrington, Saints or Widnes, so you would have three sets of lads at the game. Oldham and Castleford one year at Wigan was a cracker. There was no organisation, generally if it was Warrington or Widnes that would bring you out. Widnes always used to have a handy mob. They always came to Wigan on a double-decker bus. It had the old-fashioned open platform type of thing at the back of the bus and they would be jumping off it.

We did Saints one year at their place in a cup match in the early eighties; we put all the windows through in the pub near their ground. There were some young Wigan lads just coming through then. That was a later and completely different mob. That was when Wigan started taking it to Warrington. In the mid eighties, it was good, we would take about two hundred lads on occasion. We went to Warrington one year with a good mob and they just couldn't handle us. We were drinking in their pubs in their town centre, brilliant! After the game, where in years gone by we would have got to the station as quickly as possible, we instead marched triumphantly back to their town centre for more beers.

One year, Warrington played Barrow in a semi-final at Wigan. The Barrow lads all had these caps on with a covering going down the back of their neck like a desert hat. It was from the steelworkers at the shipyards. What they thought they looked like at the game I don't know. They had some lads amongst them, though.

Sunday afternoon in Wigan, you would have no one there. It's not like Sunday afternoons now where town centres can be quite busy, everything was shut in those days.

By the time Wigan started their Wembley run in the late eighties, I was getting a bit older and only went to a couple of the finals. I think it died out in Rugby League as far as Wigan were concerned because the Latics started being successful and there was more interest in football. Rugby League was somewhere to go for a drink on Sunday. I've been more involved at football than I have been at rugby but I've been arrested more times at rugby. I was arrested four or five times for scuffling, generally against Warrington.

Wigan were on strike once. They played the reserves side. We were away at Widnes. The week previously, there had been a television programme screened about hooligans at Millwall. Five of us got to Widnes and ended up climbing in. Where did we climb into? Right in the middle of the Widnes mob. It went off straight away. We got nicked and taken back to the station. We were let out at half-six and noticed that the floodlights were still on at the ground. We went back there and the team coach was still there. All the suited-up directors were there, they offered us a lift home so we travelled back on the team coach!

Most of us were into both Wigan football and rugby at the time. In the seventies you would definitely get lads watching Latics on a Saturday and Wigan rugby on the Sunday. Mind you, it was a lot cheaper to watch both in those days. I still watch rugby on television and enjoy it as a game. The trouble is something I've always been interested in, I've seen lads come through as eighteen and nineteen-year-olds and become main lads at Latics. I started getting involved when I was about fifteen. The thing about Wigan when I was young was that there were no lads really to look up to in that regard. I've seen it grow from nothing to what it is today at the football. I don't get involved any more but I still like to know what's going on. I like to know who's got a mob in town and so on.

I remember coming back from Coventry last year watching Latics. We were on the train and Wigan rugby had been playing Warrington. We knew they would have a mob in town but they'd grown out of it as well. They were in one of our pubs and there was no bother but there was still a dodgy, tense atmosphere. There's bound to be when you get two sets of lads in any pub. There will always be someone who could say something and spark something off, even though Latics are not really interested in rugby generally and the Warrington lads wouldn't really have a problem with Latics.

I went to Warrington the other year watching Wigan and they had a hell of a mob stood in the corner. They were in their forties like myself and I was stood amongst them. I was thinking, 'I bet these are the same lads we were brawling with twenty years ago.' They'd been out on the drink all day and were having a great time. Nothing goes on at rugby these days.

I've always been the type of person who would go anywhere. One year we were getting the train to Leeds. We changed at Manchester and who should get on the train there but a mob of around forty Warrington lads. I just thought 'Shit'. They were playing York and I hadn't thought about it previously. One of them looked over and said, 'I know you, you're fucking Wigan aren't you?' I said, 'No, I've come to York with you lads.' A lot of Leeds United lads got on at Huddersfield and were promptly leathered by the Warrington mob. The train was held up for about twenty minutes as a result. The football lads were saying, 'They're only rugby fans.' I just thought, 'You daft twats, if only you knew.'

Anyway we went to the game and I was praying these Warrington lads wouldn't be on the train coming back. Lo and behold, there they were, all hanging out the windows. I thought, 'I either risk the train or I'm going to be stuck here for a long time.' I got on and kept my head down. I could see the faces I knew come to my part of the train. They cornered me and said, 'Hey you Wiganer, you battered my brother.' Whack! They absolutely battered me. Someone pulled the cord and the guard came out. They took me into the guard's van to keep me safe. We get to Manchester Victoria and a Bobby took me off the train onto the ramp and said, 'Point out who gave you a hiding as they come off the train.' Off they came, the ones who did me. They walked past and I just let them walk past. I told the Bobby 'I couldn't see them' and let them go. If you play with fire, you get burnt. I still owe them bastards for that hiding.

In the early seventies Saints played Warrington at Central Park in a semi-final and there was a lot of trouble outside where C&A used to be. A Wigan mob was out that day too so it was lively to say the least. Wigan had gone through an alley to join in whilst Saints and Warrington were getting stuck into each other. There was loads there that day. Those days were mad because there were occasions where we didn't even go to the game. The younger elements of the mob must have passed word round school during the week that there was a chance of trouble. The older ones would just wait in the pub for the other lads' train to come in.

There was one year in the early seventies where a group of about fifty Saints lads turned up all dressed up like the characters in 'A Clockwork Orange'. Fair play to them, we were quite impressed by this mob, wearing bowler hats and light overalls. It could get very nasty between Saints and Wigan though, as shown by the year one Saints fan brought (and used) a crowbar.

In 1985, when Wigan played Hull at Wembley, I remember I was living in London at the time and had a bright yellow jacket on. This particular fashion statement obviously hadn't made its way up north yet as I was chased down the street by a horde of Wiganers oblivious to the fact that I was one of their own.

I remember 1989 at Wembley when Wigan played Saints. Well, I am saying I remember, but really I was so drunk I am relying on other people's memories of it. At first there was nothing much happening. Anyway, then we got told that St Helens had turned up and it was going off on Wembley Way. I remember smacking a couple of lads then I thought to myself 'I'm gonna get nicked here' so I packed it in. The next thing a mounted police officer is grabbing hold of me. I was chucked in the back of a police van. In the back of this van was a St Helens lad. He winked at me when I got in there. We decided to put together a story that he had seen me get arrested unjustly and he was just trying to break up the fight. We both got let off. There was loads of St Helens and Wigan lads in the nick that day who had no idea of the score of the game.

The semi-final at Man City in 1990 stands out between Wigan and Warrington. The *Manchester Evening News* featured it as there was so much trouble. It went off big time inside the ground. There was loads of Wire in the North Stand and Wigan were all in the Kippax. It started as soon as Wigan got into the ground. There were even stories that the Wire set fire to a train on the way home as it pulled into Bank Quay station.

I remember when I was young always feeling wary when we went to Warrington. There was always a very strong anti-Wigan feeling. There was one old-time Warrington face, a big man who was known as the 'Fat Man'. On the coach on the way to the game we would chant 'We Want The Fat Man'. He was almost a cult figure. We would have had no chance against him as we were only kids at the time.

One year we took a load of lads and a lot went on. A lot of shop windows got put through that day.

There was a good one against Workington at Wilderspool. It was a final so we had good numbers. When we got off at Bank Quay station, it was no surprise Warrington were waiting for us but our numbers were just too big for them.

These weren't the days of Super League where Wigan got one visit a year from Warrington, these were the days of the Lancashire Cup, John Player Cup, Challenge Cup, BBC2 Floodlit Trophy, Premiership, Locker Cup and so on. You got to know each other very, very well. The Locker Cup was the annual so-called 'friendly' fixture between Warrington and Wigan. It would annually alternate between being hosted at each town. Wigan would never go to Warrington but their lads always came to Central Park. They would turn up at one minute to three and we would be inside the ground waiting. You would be waiting for them to arrive then you would hear 'They're here'. We would make the token charge down to meet them, this would be before they'd even got in the ground! They had the numbers, they had big lads and they had the reputation.

There was a game at Odsal where Wigan played Bradford and all the Wigan lads ended up on the pitch at the end of the game. There was about three hundred of us on the pitch and the referee threatened to abandon thc game. We were having a great time sunbathing. We had ordered a double-decker bus that day to take us there.

Leeds lads turned up once when we played Hunslet. We played the game at Elland Road and with the opposition being Hunslet we weren't expecting any real bother. We got the message through that Leeds had arrived and we were shocked.

One year we played Warrington in the Lancashire Cup Final at Knowsley Road. There was a load of Wigan lads that turned up for it that day. It's one of the biggest Wigan mobs I've ever seen. We ended up on the pitch at the end of the

151

game and ran down to where the Warrington fans assembled. It ended up where they were climbing over the wall trying to get away from us. We had some cracking brawls with St Helens over the years too. I've been in Knowsley Road behind the sticks with young locals throwing half-bricks into our end from the outside.

I remember us playing Batley one year in the Challenge Cup at Burnden Park. You wouldn't think they had any boys, they were all bloody big pitmen! At first we thought it was Bolton lads turning up but it wasn't.

One year we took a coach full of lads to Widnes. Their lads told us they would meet us at a fairground on a council estate after the game. We legged them for miles. In fact, I think only four of us actually made it to the coach, leaving the rest of our lads to walk home.

We went back the following year and they came at us outside from an alleyway. I had a broken arm at the time. We stood and fought as long as we could and then we had to leg it. With being in plaster I wasn't the most mobile and I could hear them gaining on me, snapping at my ankles thinking, 'Fucking hell, this isn't going to be good.' I was right, it wasn't. They leathered me and broke my other arm. I went to the hospital and the doctor said, 'What happened to you?' I said, 'I've been to the rugby' to get the magical response, 'What are you doing playing rugby with a broken arm?' I just left it at that.

I can never remember rugby lads travelling from afar generally. You'd never get numbers of lads coming from the likes of Hull for example, although they have had somewhat of a reputation for trouble in Rugby League, as have Leigh.

I remember a Transit van filled with an insane amount of Wigan lads travelling up to Hull but they would rarely come across to Wigan in any numbers, although both Hull and Hull KR could always be relied upon to bring a handful of game lads.

Salford would never really turn up for a league match but if you got them in a semi or a final there would be a fair few of them.

Going to Blackpool for a game against Blackpool Borough was fun. I'm sure it is the law that if you go there to scuffle you will end up brawling with some random Jocks. (See earlier for confirmation.)

There was one year Latics had a twelve o'clock kick-off against Bolton at Burnden Park. As soon as the game finished we got on the bus to St Helens to see Wigan play there, quality! The same mob went to both games on the same day. Going back further, there were times you couldn't get a bus to St Helens and may have to walk part or all of the way. How times change. Now you just don't seem to get gangs of Wigan lads going to the rugby. I don't think it's as cool to be seen at the rugby as it is to be seen at the football.

It's also strange looking at the no man's land between Wigan and St Helens. I would say you've got quite a bit of Wigan support in not only Billinge but also Haydock now.

A ST HELENS SUPPORTER CONTRIBUTED THIS REPORT OF TROUBLE HE HAS WITNESSED AT GAMES.

I remember going to a game at Burnden Park, Bolton in 1986 where Saints were playing Swinton. I was only a youngster at the time and an older lad in the family took me on the coach. It was a freezing cold, dark night, typical winter rugby. I don't actually recall too much of what happened on the field but I do remember being moved around the ground due to bad trouble on the terraces. I remember looking across down to the other end of the field where gangs of lads were chasing each other round and getting stuck into each other. I was kept out of harm's way and wasn't really that frightened at the time. It was far away from me and I didn't feel bothered about it.

I never really saw much bother in the 1980s, I was a young lad anyway so wouldn't really have had any connection with such events. Having said that, I have vague recollections of seeing scuffling at Wilderspool. That was always a place that was, er, shall I say, unique. At the back of the stand, they had cockroaches so big that if you sprayed them with something they would take the can off you and spray you back.

I do also clearly recall feeling intimidated at Post Office Road in Featherstone. I saw a lad get head-butted and the blood spurted from his nose. Behind the posts were houses overlooking the pitch and I remember bottles being thrown onto supporters from those houses on occasion. The Lancashire Cup final of 1984 between Saints and Wigan was the scene of trouble. There was hooliganism at the scoreboard end of the ground, hooliganism that continued after the game with property being vandalised. At least thirty lads were getting stuck into each other at that end of the ground. They weren't kids but adults. The police just couldn't handle the numbers and force with which they were moving about. Some were obviously hammered with one old man shouting, 'Look at the state of them, they are as drunk as mops.' However, it was also clear that many of them hadn't had a drink and were involved for the hell of it. Such incidents occurred at big matches in those days and must have had an effect on the game. If you think about it, your finals are when you might get people who don't go often or even people new to the game. These incidents must have put people off and if you got caught up in it, you would be glad you hadn't taken your kids to the game.

There were also bad scenes in a Yorkshire Cup match that year when Hull KR went to Doncaster. The upshot was that Hull KR identified a handful of their own fans, circulated photos of the same to local bus companies as well as opposition clubs in an attempt to stop them getting into grounds and causing trouble. That game ended up making the national press because of unruly behaviour. Around a hundred fans made it onto the pitch. Players were confronted and then fights broke out between rival fans. When you have such numbers involved even in only isolated fights, it can be very dangerous. For one thing, there are a lot of people in a confined space and things can easily get out of hand.

There wasn't much to do really in those days. I am going to sound like an old man now but I remember when there were only three TV channels, no Internet, no mobile phones, not many computer games and nothing open on a Sunday. Rugby League was the only option on a Sunday afternoon.

Years later as a teenager, me and a few other lads would single out the Wigan away game as a good day out. Any time we drew them in the Challenge Cup at Central Park, a game inevitably shifted to a Saturday so it could be televised on Grandstand, we would head there. A group of us would get the oldest looking member of the assembled throng to get served with cans/bottles of beer/cider for us. We would then smuggle these onto a double-decker bus from the town centre to Wigan. Pretty soon, we would get rowdy, we were idiots really. We were only about fourteen or fifteen and soon got drunk and obnoxious. The language would be bad and with the lack of toilets, pretty soon rivers of piss would be flowing down the length of the bus emanating from the back. It wasn't very Christian of us that's for sure.

Off the bus and into the ground we would go, no chance of getting served in pubs. We would always try and sneak a can or two into the ground. I remember one occasion when I had two cans of XXXX down my trolleys, which were then drunk inside the ground (the cans not my trousers).

We never got into any real bother but on the way out of the ground we would often march through Wigan town centre shouting abuse at the locals before getting the bus home. The journey home wasn't always uneventful though, inevitably someone would handle their ale poorly and shoot their mouth off.

There are two recent instances of trouble at Rugby League games that I personally witnessed. The first happened in 1997 at the Challenge Cup semi-final with Saints taking on Salford at Wigan. Saints won, booking their place at Wembley and the Saints supporters walked through Wigan town centre in a jovial frame of mind. Police were giving most of the fans an escort to the station. There were hundreds walking through the streets and I became half-aware of two groups walking in front of me. On my right was a group of younger St Helens fans, I'd say they were in their late teens. On the right was a group of what I assumed to be Salford fans. It's hard to tell if they were or not though, they didn't have any colours on. They were all stocky, older fellas dressed casually. Words were definitely being exchanged between the two groups, just the normal sort of stuff after a game, you know, 'You're shit', all that stuff.

The two groups were getting closer and closer together but I noticed one skinny Saints lad sort of half-danced away from one of the blokes, backing away from him. My mate suddenly grabbed my arm and warned me, 'It's going to go off here.' You hardly ever see bother at Rugby League games so I wasn't sure. The next thing, the older blokes got straight into the young Saints group. Punches were being thrown, it was mad, it was all over in a couple of seconds. I just remember being half-pushed back as one of the stocky blokes was coming towards us. He never touched me, he was busy giving one of the young lads a slap.

Most people moved away from the bother, we ended up on the left hand side of the street. The trouble looked to be more or less over with the Saints lads lying on the floor. The last violent act I saw was a tall, dark-haired bloke booting one of the prone lads in the face. A woman shrieked at this and some blokes were saying it was out of order. Seeing it gave me that sick to your stomach feeling you get when you see someone hit when they can't defend themselves, it was bad. As we got to the station later, we saw one of the Saints lads who had been involved, his face was literally covered in blood. Later on, the mate who had warned me it was about to go off told me he had seen the older fellas say things to the Saints lads whilst holding empty beer bottles behind their back, waiting to be used against the younger lads. The police got there when it had all finished. It was over very quickly.

You'd be surprised at the type of people who used to be involved in bother. There is the assumption that people involved in organised violence are unemployed people, but a lot of lads on the scene have very good jobs and are very clever.

I remember a middle-aged fella once got hit by a young lad on the halfway line at Saints. An off-duty police officer charged at the young lad and wrestled him to the floor. At this point one of the fella's mates who looked to be in his seventies came shuffling across and aimed a sly kick at the young lad, to be told by the police officer, 'Let's have none of that.' The young assailant was carried away.

The second recent incident I personally witnessed was the last time I saw bother at a Rugby League ground. It was the first game of the 2002 season. Saints were away at newly promoted Widnes, the night was being marketed as a celebration of Widnes' return to the big time. These things never go to script though, do they? Saints won in a really tight game. There was a bunch of Widnes lads looking over to the Saints fans and gesturing. Some Saints fans were chanting things back at them. You could tell there was a bit of a bad vibe but nothing out of the ordinary. The two sets of supporters would have to get across the pitch to get at each other anyway and there was a visible police and stewarding presence. So, there was no chance of any bother. All of a sudden, and I didn't see it coming over, there was a smash and tinkle of glass. One of the Widnes lads had thrown a bottle, bang out of order as there were plenty of kids in the Saints end that night. It hadn't hit anyone directly but I could see some glass had ripped through one lad's jeans and cut his leg open. I don't think he realised so it couldn't have hurt that much. It turned out I knew a mate of the lad concerned and he didn't get much joy when he contacted Widnes after the game about it. I suppose there's not much they can do about it after the fact but you'd think they might be a bit stricter on letting people take glass bottles in with them.

It's always very rare that these things happen in Rugby League though, it's nothing compared to the football scene. I've been to games involving teams like Stoke and Cardiff City with police segregation in the stadium, and afterwards you do see big numbers of lads marching up the street, all up for trouble. It can be quite scary to be honest.

CHAPTER EIGHT

It's A Soul Thing

THE BOTHER DID change over the years, it got more violent. It went from where you would just get a bit of a kicking to where people started carrying blades. It's alright turning out for a bit of a scuffle and if someone gives you a smack, that's the gamble you take. It's a big difference though if someone is prepared to stick a knife in you. There has got to be the right sort of protocol involved. I believe some football firms don't respect firms who carry blades. They believe that it should be toe to toe, feet and hands. Realistically, if you think about it, it's going off every week across the country and you would expect people to die. It's so easy to kill somebody if someone falls and hits their head in the wrong way.

The worst kicking I have ever personally heard of was in Wigan at the Saints v Leeds Challenge Cup semi in 1994 outside a Wigan pub. A mate of a mate of mine went and told me afterwards what had happened to him. There should have been seven or eight of them going this day but because it was on telly, they found there were people crying off. A couple of them ended up going on the train. They sat behind the posts opposite the Kop end. They hung on but it turned out Saints were heading to a defeat and they headed to a pub while the game was still on. They met up with another twelve lads from town who were supposedly handy lads. They decided they would go round Wigan and went in a few pubs. At one point, some bright spark decided to ask a bloke behind the bar, 'Where's Latics today? Where do your boys drink?' referring to Wigan Athletic. They were told to try a certain pub and off they toddled. My mate told me that as soon as they left that pub, he is sure the bloke behind the bar rung their boys and told them a group of St Helens lads were heading their way.

They walked in the pub on the bar side, it was a long bar and as soon as they got in, it was on top. There were a few of their lads in and they gave them the once over. They had a beer in there and one of the lads was saying to one of the main Latics lads, 'You got battered at Maine Road off Warrington', an allegation that was forcibly refuted. Warrington had played Wigan at Maine Road in the semi-final of the Challenge Cup in 1989. I've heard both sides of this. I've heard that Warrington absolutely smashed Wigan everywhere that day but I've also heard that Wigan absolutely smashed Warrington everywhere that day. What is for sure is that it went off in the seats that day. Anyway, gradually the pub was filling up with lads and my mate realised they were going to get caned. They decided to go; my mate was one of the last out of the pub, just as he reached the door a bottle smashed into the wall above his head. They got outside and instead of standing in a line, they ended up in a sort of semi-circle waiting for the Wigan lads to come out. They came out and because of the semi-circle formation, they split the St Helens lads in two straight away. There were bottles and everything flying at them, they got pasted in that road. My mate reckons that he can honestly say he doesn't even remember throwing a punch. Most of the lads who were there got a pasting, apart from the ones who had got on their toes. They were lucky. My mate walked round looking for one of his mates with his shirt covered in blood, he found his mate and he too was covered in blood. I believe one lad got a fractured skull and at least four others suffered broken noses.

After being told of the Wigan incident, I stopped getting involved. I heard of a random, isolated incident recently that took place in a pub after a Saints game. Hand on heart, I don't know whether I would have got involved had I been there but I don't think I would. I wouldn't go back looking for it though, at all. As to the reason why I stopped, it's kill or be killed isn't it? There are more important things in life like your family, as you grow older your priorities change.

As to why the trouble stopped, it was dead weird. It was there one minute, then the next minute it had gone altogether. It's amazing when I think back, lads who you knew would be there every week then suddenly there was nobody. It's unbelievable to think at one point you could get together a mob of over a hundred lads who were up for a bit of a scuffle then suddenly it had vanished. You would go to a St Helens nightclub on a Friday night and loads of lads would say to you that they were going to go to the game and so and so was going as well, but all of a sudden it just vanished.

I've heard people explain the decline of hooliganism on the rise of Ecstasy and the whole house music culture. I'm not sure. The decline of bother certainly coincided with the rise of the dance music scene around 1988. Maybe lads who previously were getting a buzz from violence on a weekend suddenly started taking E, the loved-up drug, and getting the buzz from the pills. It certainly did have an effect. For one thing, if you were clubbing it in a chilled-out venue on a Saturday night and getting E'd up and out till six o'clock in the morning, probably only getting your head down some time in the afternoon, then why would you want to get out of your bed? Certainly not to go out on a freezing cold afternoon to watch winter rugby in the dark, standing round looking for a bit of a scuffle. Especially when the night before you've been shaking hands with everyone and telling them that although you don't know them, they're your best mate and you love them, before being told by a bouncer not to dance, you ask why and they say the magic words, 'Because the music's stopped.' The other thing is that a lot of trouble is certainly brought on by alcohol, it isn't the sole reason, but it certainly can make people aggressive.

Saints headed back to Wembley in 1996 and a few of us were sat in the pub reminiscing about old times. One of the lads talked about whether we remembered a bloke who used to go to Saints all the time, and used to take his dog to the game. The dog used to watch the game, it used to follow the ball with its head. Incidentally, the funniest thing I have ever seen in a pub happened away one year. With the help of balancing two matches on top of another match and asking one lad to try and break them with just his finger, we managed to convince said lad to set fire to his own hand. Then five minutes later, with the lad still wailing, 'Oh fuck my fucking fingers are fucking burnt' a mere two feet away, we managed to convince another lad to do the same thing. Except it took him three goes to get it to ignite properly. The comedy height of the situation was reached when the first lad punched the tiled wall of the toilet due to the pain, and badly knackered his other hand in the process.

Anyway, we decided that Wembley would be one of our last trips out and if it happened, we'd be up for it and get stuck in. There were only seven of us who went in a minibus. Most of the lads had been out the night before so had, shall we say, a little pick-me-up in the morning to help them on their way. There may even have been cases of some lads having a line or two for breakfast. One lad was skinning up all the way down. Everyone was mellow when we got there, one lad had taken his medication of a couple of happy tablets so didn't really care if we won or lost. We drove down and got there really early and headed to Euston to see if there was anything happening there. There were about twenty-five lads from town who had gone down on the Friday night. They had been up to general mischief in

Soho. They looked like they could have all done with a wash, the scruffy fuckers.

We waited for a bit but nothing was happening so we headed to the ground. One of my mates watched the game in a very happy state of mind due to the pills he had taken. He was very pleased with himself. I have to say it wasn't peer pressure that made me get involved in trouble.

It was a tribal thing. Even though I didn't watch the rugby, in effect you felt that you were fighting for and representing your town. It's a territorial thing. We had some really good laughs doing this, like when you're giving someone legs. We had some shit times as well, like when you were getting legged for example and you knew that if you got caught you would get a pasting. You're close to the people you've fought with because they've watched your back. It's pointless being in a boat with someone who's not going to row.

I do regret my involvement in the scene though. My incidents were only lads having a scuffle but others I saw, when I think back to them, I just think about how bad it was at the time. I can only look at it from my point of view, the isolated incidents I have seen. I think to myself that I should never have been involved in any of it. It's not a good thing. I'm a family man now and that's what is important to me, more than anything else. I've got too much to lose these days.

There's the common misconception that hooligans were all on the dole. It's just not true, most lads were smart and had good jobs. No idiots were involved. You had to have a bit of nous about you to be involved; you had to be streetwise. Everybody I knew was working. That's another reason hooliganism isn't as prevalent nowadays. The risk outweighs the act. You lose everything, it's not a young lad's thing. Your football lads who are into it are in their thirties and forties. The authorities are coming down on you like a ton of bricks. Imagine being tugged for affray, you've got a wife and kids, you don't come home that night because you're locked up. Your employers find out about it and you get sacked. You also get jailed. You lose everything for the sake of giving someone a dig and shouting, 'Let's get into them' in the middle of the street. It's just not worth it.

It stopped happening in Rugby League, it died a death. You don't get it in Rugby League anymore and I'm glad you don't. Imagine going to a game and there's four of you, there are ten or fifteen lads round you and you know they want to kick the shit out of you. How can you relax and watch the game? You can't do it, you wouldn't be able to relax. I've been in that situation, it's really unpleasant. The only thing worse than getting your arse kicked is waiting to get your arse kicked. It spoils the whole day, that type of incident. It's not right. People say that life is really violent now but it's not as violent as it used to be. It was going off all the time round town. There was no CCTV about then so a lot of stuff wouldn't get caught. Now it is all recorded on camera. How many coppers would you need to stop it happening back then? Every week you would leave the nightclub and there would be blood on the floor. It would be going off everywhere every weekend. People say it's gone up but that's only because more of it is reported now, but I think it's always happened and it's always been constant. It was going off at the rugby every week as well. The grog played its part because there were no all-day openings, so you would get kegged-up in a short space of time.

I think 24-hour licensing will reduce a lot of trouble. Think about it, at the moment, last orders comes and everyone downs a few drinks quickly, they then all head out at the same time to the same kebab houses and the same taxi ranks. And people are surprised that there's trouble! When we get 24-hour licensing, it will stagger (pardon the pun) the times that people decide to go home. Having said that, if it does come in I wouldn't want to be a taxi driver.

At the end of the day though, if you've got two lads who want to have a bit of a scuffle, you're not going to stop them. Young lads in large numbers gathered in a public place is a situation that is always going to have the potential for violence. It's in man's primal nature. It's a tribal thing.

Rugby League is now all about the family though, which is as it should be. Any potential flashpoint is now well-policed. In the early days when it was going off at the rugby, there were hardly any coppers there. Mind you, even at the semis that were well-policed, we always found some way of getting away and being involved in a fracas. If you look round at a game today you are surrounded by women and kids.

The incidents I have recalled in this book are my honest recollections. If you remember any of them differently, that's fine, we all have our own memories, our own perception, our own view of an event that determines the facts or fiction of the story itself.

There are a lot of football hooligan books on the market. As you have read in this book, the Rugby League hooligan activity was nowhere near the extent to that described in the football books where hundreds and hundreds of lads are involved in incidents. There were less people involved in Rugby League and it makes me wonder if what I saw in the late 70s and early 80s was happening in any normal town in England at that time. As I've said, it wasn't a Rugby League thing, that just provided a location. Maybe other towns who didn't have RL teams scuffled at their local football ground or some other convenient place.

Perhaps what was happening in Rugby League at the time was just what was happening generally around the country at the time. What is the reason for hooliganism, the so-called 'English disease' which actually is a situation that occurs all over the world? Why does it happen in our country? Is it an Anglo Saxon thing? Is it a lad thing? Is it a testosterone thing? Is it down to England being a warrior nation not just through its extended history with empire building and involvement in conflict but on an insular level going back through recent history. Consider the teddy boys in the 50s and the mods and rockers in the 60s. At the end of the day, as uncomfortable a thought as it may be, is hooliganism a part of our culture?'

Being honest, if I had a choice between music and rugby I would choose music every time definitely. Music is a massive part of my life. I get more pleasure out of it, it's there all the time, it's always around me. There's no letdowns with it, no ups and downs. I love going to the events I occasionally go to where everybody is really into their music, there are no attitudes and everyone is friendly. At the end of the day, it's not a race for money, it's a race against time. From when I was really young and I had a picture of Diana Ross and the Supremes on my wall, music has been a part of my life, it's a mind, body and soul thing. I've always been into it. Music never lets me down; it's always there for me.

BEN SMITH, A SYDNEY ROOSTERS SUPPORTER, WROTE THIS ACCOUNT OF THE NIGHT IN MARCH 2004 WHERE VIOLENCE AT A RUGBY LEAGUE GAME WOULD END UP ON THE FRONT PAGES OF THE SYDNEY PRESS THE NEXT DAY.

The aggro started early on the night the Roosters thrashed the Bulldogs, if not the violence. Walking in, the three or four young Bulldogs supporters, late teens, began to chant, 'Roosters! Roosters! Whothafuck-are-Roosters?' The biff held off for sixty minutes of one-sided Rugby League. The brawling itself must have started somewhere, obviously, but - like always with these things - no one saw it happen. Still, it wasn't hard to figure out why. The vitriol hadn't all been one-way traffic.

There's a long-running government advertising campaign in Australia aimed at rubbing out sexual assault against women. 'No means no' is the slogan. But the creative minds behind the campaign probably never imagined it being bellowed by a high-spirited lad in the terraces of the Sydney Football Stadium, also known as Aussie Stadium due to an advertising deal with Aussie Home Loans. In public opinion, this much smoke could only have equalled fire. Hands down, the Bulldogs were the most vilified club in Rugby League. Queensland police eventually decided not to proceed with charges against up to six unnamed players who had been linked to an alleged sexual assault/group sex incident on a pre-season trip to Coffs Harbour. Slurs came quickly to our lips.

And tonight - tonight - the Sydney Roosters were on their way to a humiliating 35-0 victory in the clubs' first meeting of 2004. Well into the second half, with twenty minutes to go, the Dogs had a try disallowed by boom youngster Sonny Bill Williams. He was held up over the line. The video ref flashed his call up on the big screen, and the blue and white boys in the stands seethed. The violent ones weren't there so much for the footy as for the victory anyway; the thrashing the Tricolours were dishing out was a bitter, angry pill. They had a recent history of post-game ructions. The letters blinked a mocking red taunt: No try. NO. 'No means no,' the bloke in front of us was yelling, cheering like a loon in his Roosters shirt. 'Hey, ****** No means no! Ha ha!' He followed this by glancing over at the nearby Bulldogs supporters sat sullenly across the way and cupped his ear as if to say, 'Why are you so quiet?'

'Shut up,' hissed his mate, looking furtively sideways like a criminal hiding silverware in his trousers, 'those Bulldogs blokes are gunna start belting people in a minute.'

There was violence in the air, floating through the stands like the fug of steaming midwinter breath not yet upon Sydney. It was only March, after all. Wrapped in the personal high of victory, the Roosters fans - a few of them full of lip - didn't know what was happening until it was too late. Somewhere around Bay 36 - not far from the usual 'chook pen' of the Roosters' most dedicated fans, but tonight thick with their rivals - a scuffle broke out. It was relatively minor at first, maybe three or four throwing punches, and the same again at the edges, and others trying to get out of the way as they spilled sideways and backwards over the fixed rows of seating. We were a bay-and-a-half away, and slightly closer to the field - maybe 20 metres or so, and it was not a bad laugh, really. Angry voices and shouting, a bit of blood. Good stuff. Well, shocking, really. But still. Not unexpected.

The Dogs had also been kicked out of the NRL competition in 2002 due to a newspaper's exposé of the club's massive flaunting of the salary cap; favourites for the title at the time, the Sydney Roosters had surged through the finals in their stead. Deprived of a match-up against their natural rivals, the Roosters obliterated the New

Zealand Warriors in the 2002 Grand Final. The Bulldogs always thought the title ought to have been theirs.

Tensions between the clubs and their fans - always close to the surface at any rate, due to the Roosters' 'silvertail' glamour club image clashing with the Bulldogs' roots in the mean concrete back blocks of western Sydney - were further heightened. The Roosters were the pretty boys, supported by the beautiful people of the sunny, beachside eastern suburb of Bondi, so it went. The Bulldogs were uncouth thugs from the west, building a huge supporter base among the Lebanese-dominated Middle Eastern immigrants of the area. Their supporters - at least the violent ones - were cheeky, angry young men, obsessed with gyms and machismo. Bollocks, most of it, but with a grain of truth large enough to encourage roughly the same levels of aggressive sledging the Australian slip cordon might greet Osama bin Laden with if he strolled out to open the batting at the MCG. Oz doesn't have a hoolie culture, so most fans have grown to be thick-skinned. Scuffles aren't uncommon, but someone is normally ejected and that's it. Mostly, if anything is said at all, you just sit there and take it and then shake your head and mutter a bit. The Bulldogs have a reputation for unruly behaviour from an element of their supporters. Nine fans were banned for life after a game at the Sydney Showground where they were defeated 34-6 by the Brisbane Broncos. There was crowd violence at the match and afterwards there were problems on the trains taking supporters away from the venue.

THE FAMILY GAME

I was with four English boys watching the game, all of us supporting Easts, as the Roosters are traditionally known (Bondi Beach is the English backpacking enclave of Sydney; its pubs ring out with Pommie voices like a guttural, pissed-up Westminster Chapel Choir...so not much like a Westminster Choir at all. But, still...) There had been a bit of a different atmosphere even whilst queueing up for tickets before the game. Normally, at League games the atmosphere is very good-natured and jovial. This was not the case on this evening, there was something hanging in the air. Some sort of intangible, heavy feeling that something unpleasant was going to happen. The Bulldogs were undefeated going into the game, though the Roosters' own form was up and down. The Belmore boys in blue and white were confident of doing us over. By 9p.m., the hapless Bulldogs hadn't so much been put to the sword as put to every sort of sharpenable metal utensil imaginable, in quick time. In the stands, almost bang on the hour of 9p.m., came the first flurries of punches. It went on for five minutes or so, the police trying to wade in through the throng and ejecting whoever they could identify. Just when it began to die down, the Roosters scored again. A Roosters supporter, wholly uninterested in the knuckle and simply carrying his empty beer-carrying tray back up to the bar for a refill, turned to see what the crowd had been cheering. Seeing that his team had run in another one, he cheered as well, nothing more than a semi-excited, fist clenching 'Wha-hey!'.

Unfortunately, he was right beside where the previous ruckus had momentarily backed off. We saw the punch coming before he did; a solid, twentyish-year-old man with blonde-dyed tips in his cropped hair rose and planted a straight right directly upon the fellow's thirtyish-year-old jowls, and he recoiled in the expected fashion. An affronted bystander jumped in, and he got something similar, and then it was on; mothers tried to shelter their kids (two young girls were seen on the front page of Sydney's *Daily Telegraph* in the following days, cringing a few rows away as the fighters wheeled around). Blood erupted from one round, balding face as two men began battering him; his whole face was crimson. A larger lad - huge, in fact, an Islander bloke and regularly Rooster carouser - came bounding over seats to try and break it up. He came to almost every game, a familiar face but by no means a pure footy fan, not there to sit in studied contemplation of a game. He was there to goad opposition supporters as much as to cheer on his team, a bit like the angry men he was charging towards, and often seen standing on his plastic chair and gesticulating at his rivals. He roared as he bounded up the rows of seats two by two, swearing and shrieking and careering into what was now over half-a-dozen busy blue and whites.

The Bulldogs boys were variously clinging together and being held apart, swinging punches when winding-up room or a target's head presented itself. Only two or three angry but surprised Tricolours were fighting back; mostly they were trying to break it up, and a few unrelated Dogs fans were attempting something similar. But it was useless. The big Islander boy claimed he'd barrelled in to break it up as well, I heard him say later, but he ended up banging chins - one, two, three, swinging like Frank Sinatra in a cable car. The Bulldogs boys were coming from everywhere, on mobile phones to pals, calling in for extras, kicking strangers who fell. They were belting anyone who looked like they might have been up for it, and a few who weren't; security guards, cops, Roosters supporters, others in Bulldogs colours who'd entered the fray, disgusted, to help a victimised stranger. By now, everyone was on their seats and watching the spreading brawl. No eyes were on the pitch; Roosters captain Brad Fittler could have stood on the halfway line and blasted the referee with a flamethrower and no one would have noticed (although the referee himself might have had something to say about it; probably 'Aaaaargh!').

Like spot fires, the violence in the lower level bays 36 and 37 soon flared up elsewhere. A fat man in the overhanging tier, directly above our heads, leaned over and emptied a whole plastic schooner of beer at some (imagined or real) group below. He slammed his fists into the advertising hoarding, beckoning to the fans below to 'come on, come on'. Ungainly and drunk, he almost toppled forward with the passion and the effort and, still shouting, stumbled backwards. It was good fortune and good timing when he did, as a full and sealed Coke bottle sailed at tremendous pace from the lower terrace and missed his nose by an inch; had it connected, I'd no doubt he'd have toppled over the rail and killed someone in the bay below. He was instead being lambasted with drunken chants of 'You fat bastard'. A serious brouhaha was kicking off in the stand behind him, and the brawling Bulldogs thugs in the lower stand got wind of it. In a flash they were surging upwards, en masse.

Now, smallish men and women are good at a great many occupations; for a start, the racing industry would be lost without them. But whichever careers adviser steered the two crowd-controllers in the upstairs bay towards their professions had done them a considerable disservice. The pair - a tiny blonde woman and a pint-sized man who couldn't have been more than 5' 6" - were in the thick of it. You couldn't knock their bravery. On the other hand, for all their effectiveness, they might as well have saved themselves the trouble of going out and thrown themselves down a flight of steps at home.

She wasn't so much set upon as brushed violently aside as she tried to break up a set-to, and her colleague went in to help; in a flash, three lads had him pinned and were battering him mightily. None of them would have outweighed him by less than ten kilos, and the largest by significantly more. The stand around them was clearing, but the police were presumably tied up in other affrays, and more and more Dogs boys were arriving by the moment. Then another huge supporter came to the rescue. Balding, but enormous, he was wearing a green and altogether distasteful

Hawaiian shirt and looked like a trucker or an ex-wrestler, with a neck thick enough to make looking sideways a luxury. He clouted two of them and grabbed the last - and unfortunately for him, the smallest - man by the collar. Then, with his momentum and height advantage, he pushed him backwards and three rows down, crushing him into a fixed chair. From the bottom tier we could see along the line of the larger man's arm. His fist was cocked beside his ear, and for a second he debated whether to unload or not. Then he battered him, pistoning his fist five or six times. Each one caught him flush in the face, which changed shape from the third or fourth shot and brought a groan from our level. Even when the brawling began to subside, other Bulldogs fans crowding behind the goalposts at the other end of the field took their opportunity to hurl bottles and rubbish at the Roosters players and on the field in general, forcing referee Tim Mander to pause play for a while. The Roosters supporters took advantage of this unexpected lull in proceedings to chant 'Bulldogs are wankers'.

'This is great!' said Charlie, one of my English mates, who'd completely given up watching the whitewash on the pitch over ten minutes ago. 'Does this happen all the time? I should come to the League more often!'

After the game, mind, not everyone felt the same. Throughout the week the controversy dominated the front page of the Sydney papers. The universally-respected Bulldogs captain Stephen Price was reported commenting on the ruckus in the terraces: 'It wouldn't have been a perfect situation - obviously [with] the scoreline our supporters would have been very upset and disappointed with our performance, but we just can't have that kind of thing happen,' he said.

The ABC put it succinctly, interviewing a Roosters supporter called Andrew White who had attended the blockbuster Friday night fixture with his family. He echoed the disgust of many letter-writers and talkback callers, vowing never to attend another game involving the Bulldogs. Many of the callers were disgusted Bulldogs fans. 'This has actually really scared us,' White told the Australian national broadcaster. 'My children and I actually witnessed fifteen violent attacks on different people at the end of the game. We've never seen anything like this in our lives, the amount of violence and aggression and hysteria after the game was just unbelievable.'

Roosters marketing manager Richard Fisk was quoted as saying that the violence had not been totally unexpected.

'We spent an extra $10,000 on security for tonight,' he said. 'But you can't legislate for idiots. We have worked our guts out for eight years to make this a user-friendly ground - and now this happens. One good thing about having so much extra security [around] is that there are plenty of people to take charge when these things happen.'

Police reckoned that around forty people were involved, but made only two arrests, and another seven were ejected from the ground. Local Surry Hills police set up a task force to try and sort the incident out, and to identify assailants from video footage. Bulldogs officials threatened life bans. They had only limited success.

Come Grand Final day that year, the Bulldogs played the Roosters again, in slight rain and in front of 90,000 fans. That time, and generally against the run of the public's wishes, the boys from the eastern suburbs lost their composure, dropped the ball too much and were on the wrong end of a contentiously disallowed try just before half-time. The game went down to the wire. But the Bulldogs won.

There was not a jot of crowd violence.

CHAPTER NINE

Tackling Racism

WHILST VIOLENCE in Rugby League is a thing of the past, what reared its head in early 2005 - once again imitating what has happened in football recently - is the spectre of racist abuse.

On Saturday, 15th of January 2005, an amateur rugby league match in West Yorkshire was abandoned after supporters shouted racist abuse at a black player. Shockingly, the situation then erupted into brawling and allegedly the firing of an air rifle.

These scenes occurred at amateur club Chequerfield's ground in the Pontefract area of Yorkshire during their third-round GMB Union National Cup match with the West Bowling club from Bradford. Problems began when some of the around 80-strong crowd allegedly chanted racist abuse from the touchline at the West Bowling winger, Lee Innes.

Apparently, the referee advised the player to move to the opposite wing to get him away from the supporters abusing him. It was then that, unbelievably, it appeared that an air rifle was being fired at players from a car parked at the side of the pitch.

The referee, Alan Cuttell, was forced to stop the game until the car left and then twice more halted the game as angry supporters invaded the pitch. He finally abandoned the match when fans invaded the pitch for a third time to try and attack the West Bowling players.

Glenn Barraclough, the coach of West Bowling rugby club, was quoted as saying: 'About 10 of their supporters came running on to the pitch, including women, and started attacking our players. There was a bit of pushing and shoving between two players near their dugout and the fans got a bit excited and wanted to join in.

'My players had to defend themselves. It was scary. We play in the National Conference League, where discipline is excellent. In my 22 years in the game, I have never seen anything like this. It was like a trip back into the dark ages.'

The incident was investigated by the British Amateur Rugby League Association. Maurice Oldroyd, who chairs Barla, said the organisation was very proud of its attitude towards racism and was 'very concerned'. He was quoted as saying: 'These sort of incidents are to be deplored in the strongest possible terms. We are proud of our record in rugby league football and we are one big family. Whether you are black, white, Chinese or Eskimos - sport is sport.'

Richard Mann, Chequerfield's secretary, promised to take any necessary action. He described the perpetrators as 'morons' who had been under the influence of alcohol.

He stated that the club had launched its own inquiry into the incident and, furthermore, he stressed that if any of the individuals concerned were members of the club, they would be banned. He said the problem was that it is a council-owned playing field so anyone could walk on and cause trouble.

West Yorkshire Police said it was not investigating because the events had not been reported to it.

Whilst an extreme example, sadly this type of racist behaviour is not that rare an occurrence in some areas at the amateur level of the game. One article in an issue of the Rugby League magazine *The Greatest Game* was devoted to the problem.

At the top level of the game, thankfully racism is not a problem. Where in the 80s black players were abused and the dreaded monkey chants could be heard, that was more of an issue with society at the time rather than a Rugby League-specific issue. Rugby League has a fine tradition of black players, such as superstars like Ellery Hanley and Martin Offiah. Fifty years before the first black footballer played for England, Jimmy Cumberbatch was scoring tries for the England rugby league team. In the 1950s, Roy Francis became the first black professional coach in any British sport. And in 1972, Clive Sullivan lifted the World Cup for Great Britain as the first black player to captain a British national side. It was the first sport to have a black man as coach of a British national team when the aforementioned Hanley coached Great Britain in 1994. The flamboyant Offiah sometimes faced problems in the sport from supporters, though. It is alleged that after he scored a try in one game, the supporters of the other team hurled bananas onto the pitch at him.

Nowadays though, any supporter coming out with a racist statement or behaviour at a game faces ejection from the ground and strong disapproval from supporters around him.

The game itself has taken measures to deal with the issue. In 1996, after a Leeds Metropolitan University study found a small but significant problem with racism in the game, the Commission for Racial Equality and the Rugby Football League launched the "Tackle It" campaign to challenge racism in the sport. The campaign included a 13-point action plan for professional rugby league clubs to adopt and in 1998 the Rugby Football League became the first sport governing body to formally adopt an equal opportunities policy. The 13 point plan was:

1. Clubs will formulate a statement, to be published in each match programme and displayed on permanent noticeboards around their grounds, to the effect that they will not tolerate racism of any kind and will take specific action against spectators who engage in racist chanting.

2. Clubs will undertake to prevent spectators who indulge in racist chanting or abuse from attending matches at their grounds.

3. Clubs will make public address announcements during matches to condemn any racist chanting which arises,

and to warn that swift action will be taken against offenders.

4.   Clubs will engage season ticket holders in a contract which forbids them from taking part in racist chanting.

5.   Clubs will ensure that there is no distribution of racist literature in or around their grounds.

6.   Clubs will insist upon a code of conduct for players and officials which prohibits them from making racially abusive remarks against anyone.

7.   Clubs will maintain communication with other clubs RFL headquarters, through a nominated club officer, to facilitate the effort to keep racism out of the game.

8.   Clubs will maintain a strategy for dealing with racism and abuse, and will ensure that all active stewards and, where necessary, the police are aware of their responsibilities and courses of action in this regard.

9.   Clubs will ensure that all parts of their grounds are entirely free from racist graffiti.

10. Clubs will adopt an equal opportunities policy in the areas of employment and service provision.

11. Clubs will undertake to co-operate to their best endeavours with such other groups and agencies as seek to promote awareness of race issues and to combat racism in all levels of society.

12. Clubs will ensure that their development strategies are positively weighted to

encourage the playing of rugby league, particularly at junior and youth levels, among such black and ethnic minorities that are included within their catchment areas.

13. Clubs will ensure that their youth, community and general development programmes conducted in accordance with the RFL's "framing the future" policy document reflect the needs of such black and ethnic minorities within their catchment areas.

The campaign included initiatives to help attract young ethnic minority players and spectators to the game and an emphasis on the contribution that players from ethnic minority backgrounds have made to the sport over the years.

With the January 2005 incident fresh in the mind, it is hoped that this 'disease' is not creeping back into the game of Rugby League or British society as a whole. On the whole though, the sport does not have a problem with racism and it can be truthfully said that the air rifle incident is an isolated incident within the sport.

Rugby League books from
The Parrs Wood Press

One Summer - Romance, Redundancy and Rugby League in the 1980s by Geoff Lee

The Petition - Rugby League fans say "Enough is Enough" by Ray Gent

Bamford - Memoirs of a Blood and Thunder Coach by Maurice Bamford

One Spring - Romance, Rock 'n'Roll and Rugby League in the 1970s by Geoff Lee

One Winter - Romance, Rock 'n'Roll and Rugby League in the 1960s by Geoff Lee